Purchased under Title IV-B, P. L. 93-380
Property of Painesville Township
Local Board of Education

The Dream Book

The Dream Book
OLGA LITOWINSKY
BEBE WILLOUGHBY

Illustrations by Donna Diamond

Coward, McCann & Geoghegan, Inc. · New York

RIVERSIDE HIGH SCHOOL
LIBRARY

Text copyright © 1978 by Olga Litowinsky and Bebe Willoughby
Illustrations copyright © 1978 by Donna Diamond
All rights reserved. This book, or parts thereof, may not be reproduced in any form without permission in writing from the publishers. Published simultaneously in Canada by Longman Canada Limited.
10214 • ISBN 0-698-20427-1
CIP Data appears on page 125
Printed in the United States of America
Typography by Jane Breskin Zalben

For CWAC, who showed us what to do with dreams

We wish to thank our friends, relatives, and other people who so freely shared their dreams with us, particularly Edward Babun, Calvin S. Hall, Mimi Jones, Gregory Lalire, Jim Litowinsky, Sharon Lli, Steve Mooser, Richard H. Moss, Jr., Susan Sayre Verner, and Karen Shaw Widman.

Preface

This book is based on a wide variety of sources, reflecting the eclectic nature of dream interpretation. Sigmund Freud, of course, is the father of modern dream analysis, and Freudian concepts still predominate in academic-based programs. We have relied heavily on Freud's work as well as that of Carl Jung, since Jung's goals and methods have also greatly enriched dream analysis, and the adherents to his methods have been growing more numerous during the last decade or so. In addition, new explorers of dreams have emerged over the years, many of whom recognize that no single theory can explain all the levels of meaning in dreams. Although it is impossible in a book of this size to cover all the new approaches, we hope we have highlighted those ideas we feel are most important.

Dreams can be baffling, indeed, but many are accessible to the person who earnestly desires to understand himself or herself. Our own experiences have shown us that the best guides to the meanings of dreams are the feelings of the dreamers who trust themselves enough to listen to their nocturnal voices and bring to light what they already know to be true.

—O.L. and B.W.

The Dream Book

Contents

1 · Mushrooms in His Bed 15
2 · Hundreds of Steps 21
3 · Inner Journeys 29
4 · Once upon a Pyramid 39
5 · A Night of Dreaming 49
6 · Fire and Snakes 57
7 · Pictures on Water 65
8 · Living Is Not Easy 73
9 · Fears in the Night 81
10 · Psychic Dreams 89
11 · The Dream People 97
12 · A Dream Journal 107
     For Further Reading 117
     Sources 119
     Index 123

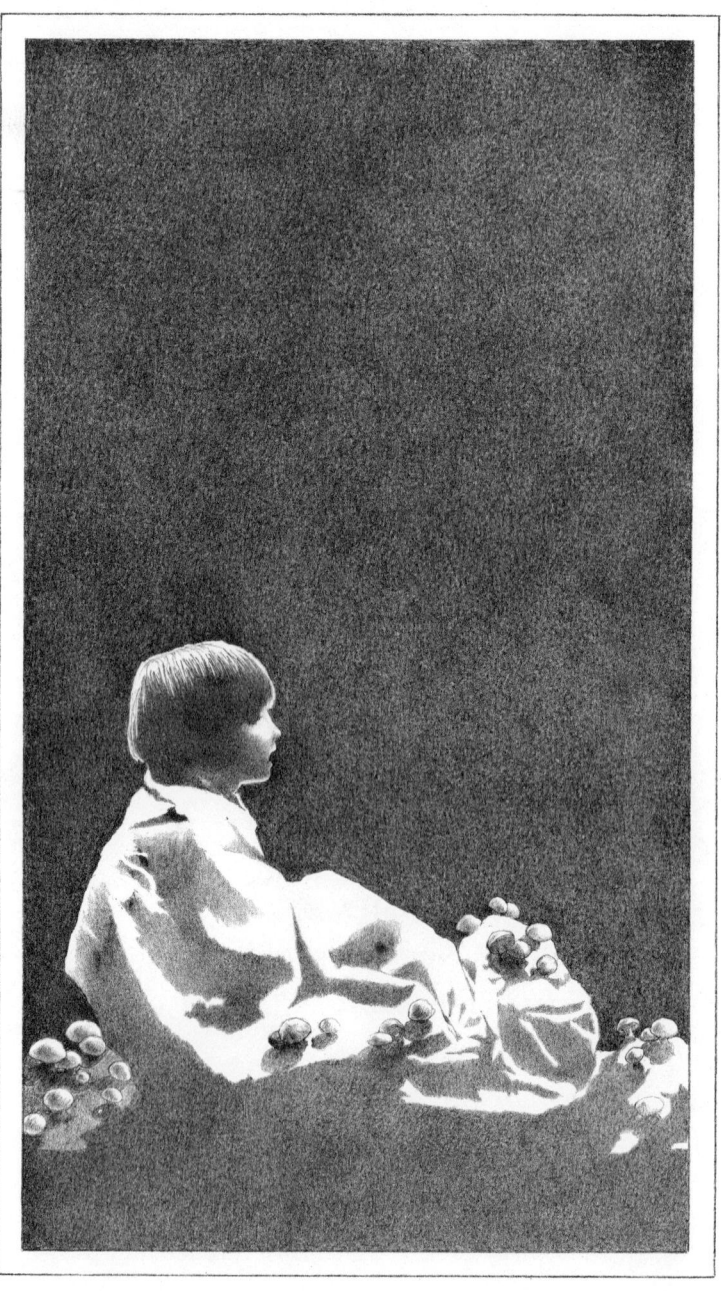

1 · Mushrooms in His Bed

I woke up in the middle of the night and screamed: "Mama, Mama, my bed is full of mushrooms."

Gregory

Every night, soon after you have fallen asleep, you set out on a bizarre journey along a strange road, which twists and turns unpredictably. Places and people may keep changing. A mist may seem to surround everything; nothing is solid. You never know where the road will lead you or what you will see on this long journey through the mysterious night world you sleep in. You are dreaming.

It is different when you are awake; then you can daydream whatever you like. You can be Wonder Woman or Superman, explore a desert island or beat up the class bully. Although your daydreams may be truly fantastic—another word for daydream is *fantasy* —you can control them and change your daydreams any way you like. Night dreams are not like your daytime fantasies because for the most part a dream is not under the control of your conscious mind. Dreaming is a special way of thinking when you are asleep.

Every healthy person dreams every night—even babies. Although some people say they never dream, sleep researchers—scientists who study sleep—have not found any normal person who does not dream. As far back as there are records, there are reports of dreams. Through the ages, in all times and places, people have been puzzled by dreams and have tried to explain why we dream. Long ago kings would even hire dream "experts," who were supposed to know why certain dreams were dreamed at certain times.

And people have sometimes wondered whether dreams were real, whether they had separate lives of their own. A man named Chwang-tse once wrote that he dreamed he was a butterfly, but when he woke up he at first did not know whether he was a man dreaming he was a butterfly or whether he was a butterfly dreaming it was a man.

Dreams do have a life and logic of their own; they happen. But are they real? Chwang-tse did dream he was a butterfly, but he was really a man, because it was as a man that he wrote about being a butterfly. There is no proof that the butterfly continued to exist after the dream was over.

Sometimes it is hard to believe that dreams are not actually happening because they seem so real, as when Gregory dreamed there were mushrooms in his bed.

"*I woke up in the middle of the night and screamed: 'Mama, Mama, my bed is full of mushrooms.'*"

There were no mushrooms in the room, but the dream had been so vivid that for a few moments Gregory believed they were still in bed with him. A frightening dream like this is called a nightmare.

It is important to remember that the butterfly and the mushrooms existed only in the minds of the dreamers. Our dreams are created by ourselves and nobody else. They show us that our sleeping life can be a time of great richness of imagination, *our* imagination. Our dreams are also the keys to unlocking a secret part of ourselves called the unconscious.

It is impossible to draw a picture of the unconscious or to say exactly where in the brain it is located. But if we imagine the mind to be like a house, then the unconscious might be said to be like the basement or the attic. It is a storehouse in the mind of everything we have ever experienced or felt deeply. The conscious mind is like the main floor, where most of our waking hours are spent; we know our way around the main floor pretty well.

But the unconscious is a mysterious place. It holds pleasant and unpleasant feelings and ideas we are not aware of when we are awake. These feelings and ideas may be ones we are ashamed of or afraid of, or that hurt us; they may be ones that make us feel good. Very often they are ideas and wishes we do not even realize we have. The unconscious is also a storehouse of our hidden gifts, and our dreams are the windows through which we can see them so that later we may develop them into full-blown talents. The unconscious remembers everything that has ever happened to us; it does not forget or ignore anything.

At night, when we fall asleep and start our mysterious journey, the conscious part of the mind relaxes. It is like a gatekeeper who dozes, leaving a door open to another part of the mind. Now the unconscious begins to work freely, and our unknown thoughts and feelings become dreams.

2 · Hundreds of Steps

I had to climb hundreds of steps before I got to school. It took forever. At the top of the stairway I came up against a sheet of yellow lined paper, so huge it blocked the door to the school. As I stood there, the paper suddenly tore open. A witch loomed up in front of me. I screamed.

Mimi

Suppose your friend Henry swears that he is not afraid of thunderstorms. "Thunder is caused by hot and cold air moving among the clouds," he says. Yet whenever there is a storm, Henry trembles. Even though he knows the thunder is harmless, the loud noises still frighten him—and he doesn't know why.

For thousands of years, people have suspected that "something" made them act and feel differently from the way they thought they wanted to. A man who accidentally spilled boiling water on his foot in olden times would explain it by saying, "An evil spirit made me do it." Today, most people don't believe in evil spirits, but we do know there is a part of our mind that causes us to have feelings or to do things for reasons we can't always explain. It is our unconscious.

About one hundred years ago, when people began to study the mind in a scientific way, they felt sure that there was an unknown part of the mind that influenced people's behavior, but they could not be certain of it. Sigmund Freud was one of the greatest researchers in this new science—psychology—and one of his most important achievements was his work on the unconscious.

Freud was a doctor who lived in Vienna, Austria. He treated people who suffered from mental illness, especially from a type then known as hysteria, which was characterized by physical illness, often paralysis. Freud was one of the first doctors to realize that many neurotic symptoms such as phobias, obsessions, and hysteria were caused by events that had happened in the patient's early childhood—so early and so traumatic or painful that the patient often couldn't remember them; they were repressed, that is, hidden in the unconscious. The more Freud spoke to his patients, the more he came to believe that although they tried to, people could not always tell the truth about themselves, because they didn't know it. In other words, as the English psychiatrist R. D. Laing has said, the patient forgot the incident and then forgot that she forgot it.

One way to uncover his patients' true feelings, Freud found, was by studying their dreams. He also kept a record of his own dreams as a means of studying dreams and learning more about himself. Freud eventually developed a technique known as free association. He would ask his patients what thoughts came to their minds as they talked about their dreams.

"You dreamed about a flower," he might say. "What do flowers remind you of?" "Well, I know a woman named Mrs. Bloom," the patient might reply. "She is as pretty as a flower." And so it would continue.

By freely connecting material from a dream to the memories, thoughts, or feelings it brought to mind, Freud was able to decipher the dream. He found that if a person learned the truth (even though it was painful) about a repressed incident, he might accept it, and his behavior might change or his symptoms eventually disappear. Freud was the first person to provide a method for studying the relationship of dreams and the unconscious.

The reasons dreams were hard to understand, Freud thought, was that a "censor" in the mind edited the dream to make it acceptable to the dreamer. Often the feelings were so frightening that if the dreamer felt them, he would surely wake up. "Dreams are the *guardians* of sleep and not its disturbers," said Freud.

The most important function of a dream was to express a wish, Freud believed. "A dream remains a fulfillment of a wish, no matter in what way the expression of that wish fulfillment is determined." By this Freud meant that dreams could turn desires inside out and upside down in such a way that the dreamer would not even suspect a wish was present. One of his patients dreamed that she saw a certain man at her nephew Karl's funeral. She was upset by this dream, for she did not wish Karl to die. In real life she had recently been to the funeral of Karl's brother Otto, where she had seen this man. The dream was an expression of her desire to see him again, Freud said, not a wish that Karl die.

Mimi dreamed, "I had to climb hundreds of steps before I got to school. It took forever. At the top of the stairway I came up against a sheet of yellow lined paper, so huge it blocked the door to the school. As I stood there, the paper suddenly tore open. A witch loomed up in front of me. I screamed."

In Mimi's dream she had many steps to climb to get to school, a sheet of paper blocked her way, and a witch was threatening her. This dream expressed Mimi's wish that she not have to go to school. It also told her that something about school was frightening her.

Dreams have two levels of meaning, according to Freud. The manifest content of a dream is simply a story or a series of dramatic incidents. For example, in Mimi's dream, the manifest content is the story of how she tried to go to school but was stopped by a witch. The latent dream thoughts, which underlie the story, reveal the meaning of the dream; it can be reached through interpretation. For example, if Freud used free association with Mimi about her dream, it might go like this:

"FREUD": You dreamed about a witch. What did she look like?
MIMI: She was dressed all in black, and she had pointy shoes.
"FREUD": Does that make you think of anyone you know?
MIMI: My teacher. She wears black witch shoes.
"FREUD": How do you feel about her?
MIMI: She scares me. I don't think she likes me. She's always giving us lots of homework, and we have to use yellow paper like in the dream.
"FREUD": And what else?
MIMI: School. . . . I don't like school. I wish I didn't have to go to school. I hate my teacher. She's a witch! No, no. I didn't mean to say that. *(The censor comes into play as Mimi goes on.)* My teacher isn't a witch. She's my teacher. I can't call her a witch. I'll get punished.

Since Mimi's mother and father had always told her that teachers were good people, Mimi could not allow herself to believe otherwise. Once Mimi could admit that not only was she afraid of her teacher but also did not like her, she would be closer to understanding her feelings about school. When it is hard or impossible to to domething in a dream (as it was for Mimi when she had to climb "hundreds of steps"), it usually means there's a conflict. No wonder it was so hard for Mimi to climb those stairs in her dream. She

25

knew she had to go to school—but she didn't want to.

Freud was the first man to explore the unconscious systematically by means of dreams, and he devoted his great book *The Interpretation of Dreams* to unraveling the bizarre manifest contents of dreams until their meanings could be understood.

3 · Inner Journeys

A creature—a rabbit?—was running away from me. I followed it into a dark place, a tunnel. But inside there was a woman behind a desk and books all over. I wanted to get by the woman and follow the creature, but I couldn't. I was stuck.

Sharon

Carl Jung was a psychiatrist who worked closely with Freud for many years. As a young man in Switzerland, Jung had studied philosophy and archaeology, but he chose medicine as his profession. As time went on dreams, fantasies, and mystical experiences began to interest him so much that he became a psychiatrist because this career combined the facts of science with the mysteries of the human personality.

The study of dreams must have seemed as silly early in this century as a belief in flying saucers does to many people today. Nonetheless, Jung persisted in his study of dreams, and he and Freud each developed systems for interpreting them. The two men frequently discussed their own dreams with each other. Like Freud, Jung believed there was a personal unconscious which could be tapped by concentrating on dreams and fantasies. But Jung also believed there was such a thing as the collective unconscious, which is a reservoir of all human history contained in each person's unconscious. Jung believed this explained why all men and women feel so strongly about so many of the same things.

For example, everyone was born of a mother. Even though your mother is different from everyone else's, we all share a common feeling about the idea of mother: She is the source of life. Jung called such strong emotional ideas archetypes, and he spent many years studying mythology, archaeology, and diverse cultures to discover the ideas he believed all people had in common from the day they were born. These ideas, Jung was sure, had great religious or spiritual significance.

Freud, however, could not accept Jung's concept of the collective unconscious. For his part, Jung disagreed with Freud on many points as well, and finally their friendship ended. To this day, Jung's ideas about the collective unconscious remain perhaps the most controversial part of his work.

From his study of primitive cultures, Jung came to believe that tribal people were often closely in touch with the collective unconscious, since they lived simply in a natural setting and had many customs and rituals which were related to the tribe's survival. In a culture like that of the Australian aborigines, for example, a boy on the verge of puberty is sent out to live alone in the wilderness for a year. At the end of this period, which the aborigines call the walkabout, the boy is welcomed back to the tribe, no longer a boy but a man. Not only has the boy learned to survive the hardships of the wild, he has also learned to overcome fear and loneliness and often has had religious experiences that he will use as a guide throughout life.

The walkabout in one form or another is common to many cultures that hold puberty rites. The religious ceremony of confirmation in our own day is a vestige of an older tradition in which young people were formally declared to be adults when they reached a certain point in their adolescence.

But we who live in the modern world no longer live so close to nature. We are wrapped up in the world of doing things—going to school, holding jobs, extracurricular activities, entertainment, and the like. We seem to have no time and little encouragement to listen to our inner selves or to think about what our rituals and ceremonies originally meant. We become so used to being bombarded from outside ourselves that many people find it difficult to be alone in the quiet when all the "civilized" noise is turned off.

But every night we enter one place that is exclusively ours: our dream world.

Dreams can be metaphors—poetic comparisons—for real-life situations. You are the hero in your dreams just as you are the hero of your life. As the Russian poet Boris Pasternak has said, "Life is not crossing a field." It is a journey in which you will be faced with uncomfortable or dangerous situations. You will have to make difficult decisions. At these times your inner strength and resources will help you, and your dreams are a way of preparing you just as the walkabout prepares the aborigine for his life.

Someday you, too, will have to leave your home and encounter the unknown. For some, this will be a time of high adventure; for others, it will be a time of anxiety. It may be both at once.

You may dream you have gone to the moon. Does this mean you want to be an astronaut? Or does the dream have a deeper meaning? Perhaps the bleak landscape of the moon suggests your loneliness as you face the unknown; that is, the life that stretches before you.

You may dream you are caught up in an earthquake. The ground shifts under your feet; there is no place to run. How do you, the hero of your dream, react? Do you panic or are you calm? What does this tell you about the way you handle a turbulent emotional situation in which it seems the very foundations of your world are shaken?

You may dream that you are rooted to the ground, unable to move or scream, while an invisible horror stalks you. What are you afraid of? What can you do about it?

Our dreams express the highest and lowest degrees of our spiritual side, Jung believed, and from our dreams we may learn about our innermost thoughts and feelings. We can use what we learn to grow and mature further, especially when there are obstacles to be overcome and new knowledge to be gained, as in the countless myths, legends, and folktales about heroes and their quests or tasks. A knowledge of yourself—your desires, your values, your feelings—is the most valuable weapon you can have on your own heroic journey through life.

As you read on in *The Dream Book* you will see how dreams are metaphors for situations in the lives of various people. Some may be similar to your own experiences and feelings; some may be totally different.

Hercules in the Greek myth had to perform twelve impossible labors (he finally became a god); Jonah in the Bible was condemned to be swallowed by a great fish before he could return to his people; Pinocchio was swallowed by a whale and was almost changed into a donkey before he could become a real boy. Alice in Wonderland had to overcome the obstacles encountered in an illogical world until, at the end, she could tell the Queen of Hearts and her court that they were nothing put a pack of cards. Journeys like these represent inner journeys, journeys of the spirit.

Here is an imaginary dialogue between Jung and a young girl named Sharon, which we hope will help you understand how he worked with his patients. Jung regarded a dream as an event in itself. Rather than use free association as Freud did, Jung preferred to sit patiently, like a fisherman, and try to hook an element of the collective unconscious that had a strong emotional meaning for the dreamer.

Sharon dreamed, "A creature—a rabbit?—was running away from me. I followed it into a dark place, a tunnel. But inside there was a woman behind a desk and books all over. I wanted to get by the woman and follow the creature, but I couldn't. I was stuck."

"JUNG": In the dream, you were trying to go down a tunnel.
SHARON: I felt like Alice in Wonderland. I wanted to follow that rabbit.
"JUNG": What for?
SHARON: Because there was something I wanted down there.
"JUNG": What?
SHARON: Well, Alice found a world down the rabbit hole that was different from the real world.
"JUNG": How was it different?
SHARON: It was a fantasy world. She met a lot of strange people—
"JUNG": And...?

SHARON: I'm lonely. I don't have any friends. If I can't have real adventures, I at least would like to paint them or write about them. If I could follow that rabbit—
"JUNG": The rabbit is the part of you that wants to lead you into a more exciting life.
SHARON: Yes, but the rest of me can't follow it. There's something in the way—a desk covered with books. And a woman. I can't get past them.

This dialogue technique can also be carried out alone if a person talks to himself as though he were carrying on an interior conversation with the characters in his dream. Sharon will have to learn how to unblock the passage that is keeping her from a more adventurous life, the life she claims to want. She will have to find out more about the barriers in her life—the desk, the books, the woman—that block her efforts to write and paint, and the rabbit part of her personality will have to become more confident.

One way for her to do this is to keep a record of her dreams (as explained in Chapter 11) over a period of time to see if there are further clues or a pattern in them. The same people and events keep turning up in dreams, and if there is a mistake in interpretation it will be corrected as time goes on or more dream material becomes available. Jung believed a series of dreams made the most satisfactory basis for successful interpretation.

If you follow your dreams closely you should see a change as you grow older. Jung called this a kind of growing, the process of individuation, coming to terms with your inner center, finding out who you really are, what you want, and the best way for you to live. One of Sharon's tasks is to discover what is keeping her from her goal. Jung believed that dreams are a little bit ahead of the dreamer's consciousness, and if we pay attention to them, we can discover our inner conflicts and desires.

The exploration of our unconscious life is one of the greatest adventures available to each of us today—it's natural, free, and nearby. Jung said, "It is the guide, friend, and advisor of the conscious." Through our dreams, the unconscious offers advice available no other way.

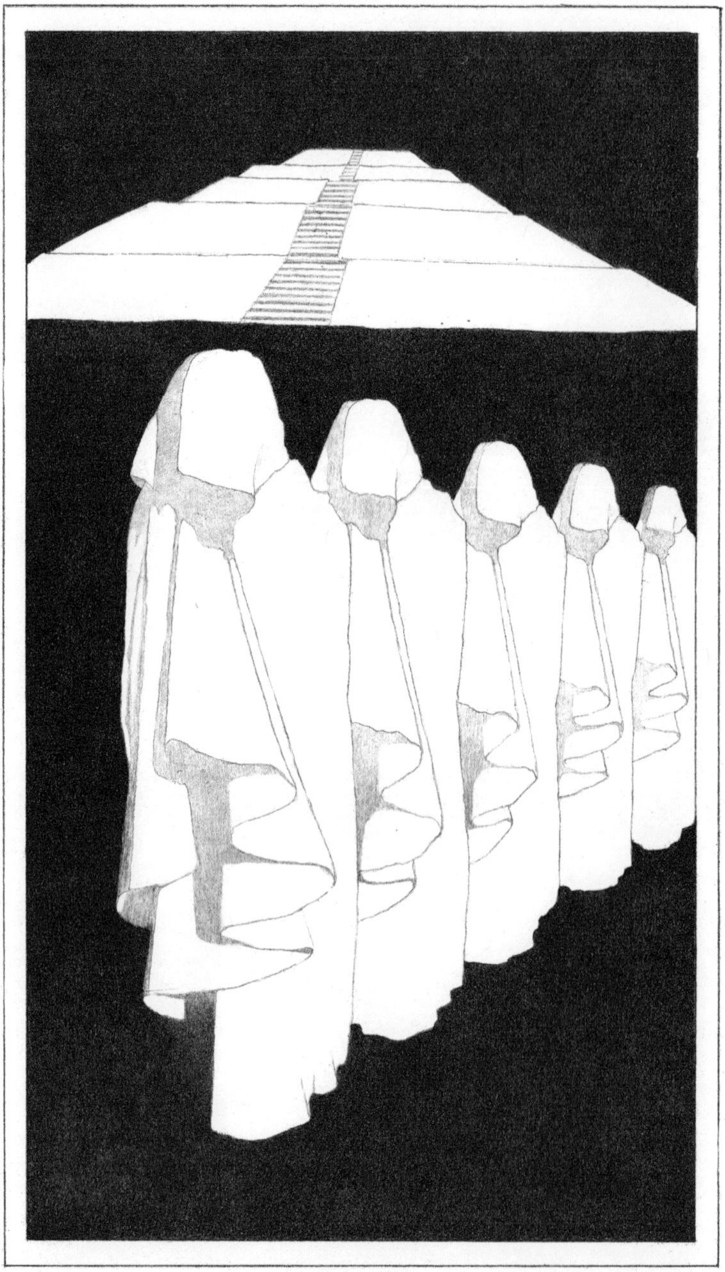

4 · Once upon a Pyramid

I watched Aztec maidens dressed in long, white robes file past me and then slowly climb to the top of an Indian pyramid in Mexico.

Mike

The Greek poet Homer called sleep and death "two twins of winged race, Of matchless swiftness, but of silent pace." And Sir Thomas Browne echoed Homer, saying in the seventeenth century that "Sleep is a death." But nothing could be farther from the truth: We are very much alive when we are asleep. Our heart keeps beating, our lungs breathe air in and out, our blood circulates, and our mind is busy. To find out just how busy our sleeping bodies and minds are, scientists have spent many long, weary nights in sleep laboratories since the early 1950s.

It was then that Eugene Aserinsky, William Dement, Nathaniel Kleitman, and others began to study the sleep of student volunteers at the University of Chicago. Sleeping and dreaming have now been charted, measured, and diagrammed to as fine a point as modern technology makes possible.

In a typical sleep and dream experiment, tiny metal discs called electrodes are attached to the head of a volunteer. Wires leading from the electrodes are then hooked up to a box attached to a wall at the head of the sleeper's bed. A cable from the box leads to an electroencephalograph, a machine that records brain waves, set up in another room.

After turning off the light in the volunteer's bedroom and wishing him good night, the researcher goes into the room where the electroencephalograph is. As the volunteer sleeps, the researcher watches rows of pens writing on a moving roll of paper called an electroencephalogram, or an EEG, where the volunteer's brain waves are being recorded. In addition, at least two electrodes are attached near the volunteer's eyes so that eye movements can be monitored by the electroencephalograph as well.

To get an idea of what the electrodes near the eyes are recording, close your eyes and place a fingertip gently on each lid. Now move your eyeballs from side to side. Can you feel eye movements beneath the lids? Next, ask a friend to close her or his eyes and move the eyeballs. Can you see them move under the closed lids?

As the student volunteers slept away the nights, the researchers noticed that when the volunteers' eyeballs moved, the rhythm of their brain waves changed. The researchers began to wake the volunteers whenever the EEG showed that the eyes were moving. Nearly every time, the volunteers reported that they were dreaming. For the first time in history it was possible to actually measure dreaming based on the rapid eye movements (REMs) of the sleeper. The discovery that REMs indicated a person was dreaming opened a whole new era in dream and sleep research. We now know a great deal more about something we all do but few understand.

All night long there are regular cycles of sleeping and dreaming, lasting some ninety minutes. Individual REM dreams may go on from ten minutes to an hour and, depending on how long the dreams are, a person will have about four or five REM dreams a night, totaling about two hours of REM dreaming for every eight hours of sleep.

When we first fall asleep, we enter a light sleep known as the hypnagogic state. If our sleep is uninterrupted, this happens only once during the night. Dreaming is fitful during these few moments, as if the brain were sorting out the last, leftover thoughts from the day, trying to decide which were worth pursuing. Eye movements are slow (SEM).

One night Mike was lying on the sofa, reading a book about Cortez and the conquest of Mexico. He dozed off and soon was dreaming. *"I watched Aztec maidens dressed in long, white robes file past me and then slowly climb to the top of an Indian pyramid in Mexico,"* he said. A few minutes later Mike's mother woke him and told him to go to bed.

If his mother had not awakened him from the hypnagogic dream, Mike would have entered descending stage 1 of sleep. His eyes would have moved slowly or not at all; this is known as NREM (for no REM). If he were awakened at this point, he would probably report that he felt as if he was drifting off to sleep.

When he was finally asleep in his bed, Mike went through descending stage 1 of sleep, and then entered stage 2, which is an intermediate or transitional phase of light sleep. He had no REMs. When he entered the next stage of sleep, stage 3, he slept lightly and could be awakened easily. But in the ensuing stage 4, he was sleeping soundly. If he were to be awakened during stage 4, he would probably report feeling confused. There are no REMs during stages 3 and 4.

At last, about ninety minutes after he fell asleep, Mike entered ascending stage 1 sleep, or the D-state. If an EEG were being made of Mike's brain waves, it would show lines that looked as if he were about to wake up. However, in the D-state, Mike would be as heavy as a log and almost as difficult to wake up. He would be having intermittent REMs during this period, and even though the EEG would show "waking-up" brain waves, Mike would probably say, if he were awakened, that he felt as though he were in a deep sleep.

At the sleep laboratories, when volunteers with REMs were awakened, they recounted detailed descriptions of dreams that were taking place. One dreamer reported that he had been throwing basketballs at a net; his eyes had been moving up and down. First, he said, he would shoot and look up at the net; then he would look down to pick up another ball. Another dreamer had eye movements from side to side; he reported that he was watching two people throw tomatoes at each other in his dream. Often, when the volunteer's eye movements were slow or nonexistent, he would report that he had been looking at something in the distance or just staring at an object. When the REMs were of various kinds, the dreamer would report that he was interacting with other people or inspecting objects close up. When there were many REMs, the dreamer's role was active; if there were few, his function was passive. In other words, eye movements often matched the action in a dream as if the dreamer were watching a movie!

As research continued, new findings began to be reported swiftly. During REM sleep, that is, while you are dreaming, your heart beats faster and you breathe more heavily. Your blood pressure rises, and if you are a male, there are erections of the penis. We may seem "dead to the world" while we sleep, but our bodies and minds are quite alive.

As far as can be estimated, babies dream more than children do, and old people dream the least of anyone. Most animals dream, or at least have REMs. If you have a pet dog or cat, you have probably noticed it twitch when it is sleeping. Next time, see if you can detect eye movements! We don't know yet if all animals dream because not all animals have been tested, but it has been observed that baby chicks have eye movements while they are still in the shell. Some scientists think eye movements in young animals and babies are related to learning, but so far the purposes of dreaming are still unknown, although there are many theories.

At first it was thought that nothing was happening during stages 2, 3, and 4, when there were no REMs. But then David Foulkes, another researcher at the University of Chicago, began to wake volunteers during the NREM stages. Instead of asking, "Tell us your dream," or "What were you dreaming about?" he simply asked if the volunteer had any thoughts at all.

Suddenly another discovery was made: people's minds are active during the NREM stages, too, but in a way that is different from during the REM stage. The volunteers reported that they were "thinking," and their thoughts were much more in tune with everyday common sense. One volunteer said, "I was thinking about this phone call from home. . . . My parents were angry with me because I haven't written." In general, the NREM "dreams" were much less dreamlike, much more like ordinary thinking, than REM dreams. It would seem that "dreaming" goes on all through the night, but in most cases, the distorted, bizarre dramas we usually think of as dreams occur only during REM periods.

Foulkes believes that the "thoughts" which occur during NREM stages are later elaborated into a REM dream. For example, during a NREM period, one volunteer reported that he had been "dreaming about getting ready to take some type of an exam. . . . I don't think I was worried." Then, during a REM period, he said, "I was dreaming about exams. . . . I had just finished an exam, and it was a very sunny day outside. It was walking with a boy who's in some of my classes with me." The same student then reported another NREM dream: ". . . dreaming about exams, and about having taken different exams."

It is clear from this series that the volunteer had exams on his mind. But something else was happening in his second dream: it was a drama, not a thought, a perfect example of a wish-fulfillment dream. The exams were over and the dreamer could enjoy himself with his friends in the sun again.

Sleep talking and sleepwalking occur only during NREMs. Sleepwalking usually takes place early in the night. There is "tossing about" almost all night long, especially in stages 2 and 3, but not during stage 4, the deepest sleep of the night.

Whatever the reasons for dreaming, it is clear that we all dream, and we can learn from our nocturnal dramas if we know how to go about it.

An Average Night of Sleeping

EEG — Awake
Sleep — Hypnagogic
Stages — Asleep descending

1
2
3
4

10   20   25   30   35

0   1   2   3   4   5   6   7   8

* Descending stage one

There are five different stages of sleep: descending stage 1 (which occurs only once during a night of uninterrupted sleep), followed by stage 2, stage 3, and stage 4. The fifth stage of sleep is called ascending stage 1 or the D-state (for Dream-state); this is when REM dreaming occurs.

On the chart the broken line refers to descending stage 1. The shaded areas indicate the REM dreams, which occur in ascending stage 1 of sleep; the numbers above them show how long a dream has lasted. The numbers at the bottom of the chart are the number of hours that have passed in sleep. From the top of one loop to the top of the next is one cycle. During the night we go through four or five sleep cycles, each of which includes all or only some of the sleep stages described.

From the chart, it can be seen that as the night goes on less time (or even none) is spent in stages 3 and 4, and the cycles may simply consist of swings between stages 1 and 2; REM dreams will last a longer amount of time toward morning.

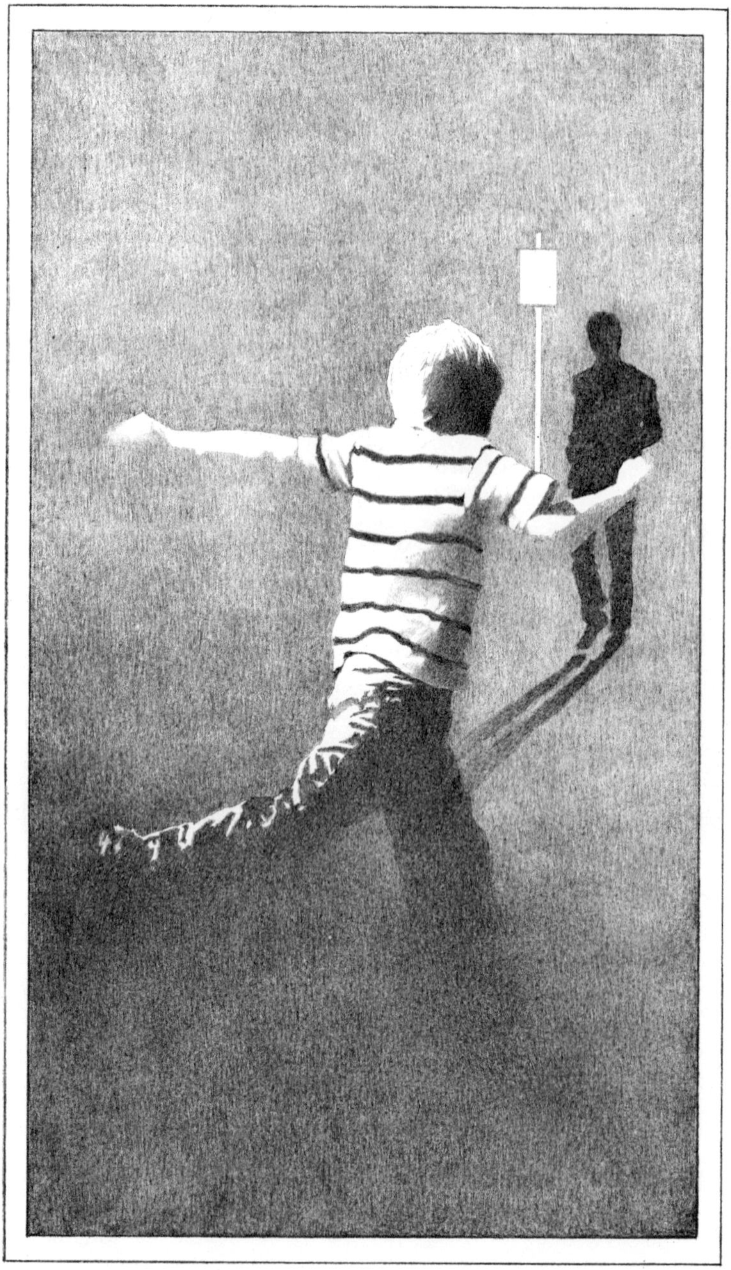

5 · A Night of Dreaming

Something was chasing me. I ran faster and faster. At last I came to a bus stop and said to the man who was waiting for me, "You're not going to believe this." I went on to tell the man all about my dream of being chased.

Steve

As the research into dreaming continued, another important discovery was made: It appears that all our dreams during the night are connected and express various ways of dealing with a problem that may be in the back (or sometimes in the front) of our minds. In other words, we spend the whole night thinking and dreaming about the same thing in various ways. Alfred Adler, another great psychoanalyst who lived at the same time as Freud and Jung, believed that dreams were a continuation of our waking life and were attempts to solve current problems. The dream's purpose was to shape the feeling that would be used the next day to confront the problems in reality. The feelings felt in the dream were the most useful guides to our waking life.

Jung was in close agreement with this view. He thought that dreams tell us what needs "adjustment." Unlike Freud, who thought that dreams were about such terrible feelings they needed to be disguised through distortion, Jung said, "The dream does not conceal; we simply do not understand the language."

But if dreams are so important, why do we have such trouble remembering them? No one has the final answer to this question, but several theories attempt to explain the reasons, which cannot be proved scientifically.

One theory is that many dreams are just not that interesting, and so a person couldn't care less about remembering them. We can usually remember nightmares or other vivid dreams. Another is that a dream may make a person feel too uncomfortable (he doesn't want to face that problem he keeps dreaming about) and so he doesn't want to remember it (in this case the forgetting is often done unconsciously). Many people wake up quickly and dash out of bed to begin the day and don't give themselves a chance to remember. It may also be that a person is not aware that dreaming is important, and he will dismiss his night experience by saying, "Oh well, it was just a dream; not really worth anything."

In addition to these psychological reasons for not remembering dreams, there is also a physical one. According to Foulkes, after a REM dream, a NREM period comes along, and the brain just hasn't had a chance to absorb the REM dream before it is "wiped out" by the next thought. If a person is awakened during or right after a dream, he'll remember it, just as most of us often remember the last dream of the night. Foulkes has a theory that the phenomenon of *déjà vu* (the feeling you've experienced something before) may be the trace of a dream you had in the middle of the night. Although you forgot it, something during the day might trigger the memory, and you'll feel, "Oh yes, that's familiar; now I remember."

A night of dreaming is like a book, and each dream is a chapter. Your dreams usually contain "day-residue" elements; that is, they use thoughts from the day to weave the night story, as Steve did in his dream.

"Something was chasing me. I ran faster and faster. At last I came to a bus stop and said to the man who was waiting for me, 'You're not going to believe this.' I went on to tell the man all about my dream of being chased."

Steve dreamed this in a sleep laboratory. He was a volunteer and felt nervous about being awakened to tell his dream to a researcher. In other words, he had used thoughts from the day—the bus he took to the laboratory, the laboratory itself, the experiment—to create a dream.

Unlike the volunteers in a sleep laboratory, you may not be able to wake after each of the four or five dreams you have during a night. But don't worry, the last was the most important, as you will see from the following series.

Let's say you are worried about the fact that the bigger kids in your class pick on the smaller ones—and you're one of the smaller ones. The day before the dream night, there was an incident at school where the bigger kids pushed their way ahead of you in the lunch line and no one stopped them. That night, you and your family go to the movies and see a film about a dolphin. This is how your book of dreams might be written.

The first dream. *You dream you're at the beach and there is a long line of people waiting to go into the water.* This dream is just a dream about the events left over from the day before. The movie was about the sea which reminded you of the beach, and you had been in line at school and at the movies.

The second dream. *You dream a baby is sitting in a bathtub. A big boy comes into the bathroom and splashes her until she cries. A woman comes in and gives her some milk.* The baby is you when you were smaller; the boy is your big brother who used to tease you and make you feel unhappy; the woman is your mother (she was always giving you milk). This dream takes you into your past and reminds you of the time when you had the same feelings you have now about being small, weak, and helpless.

The third dream. *You are playing in the water with a dolphin. You climb on its back, and it swims away with you to an island where there is candy growing on trees. When you land on the island, friendly boys and girls come running up to welcome you.* This dream is an "escape" or wish-fulfillment dream. You are far away from the classroom, and your new companions like and respect you.

The fourth dream. *A giant barracuda-octopus is chasing you. It is the ugliest, most terrifying monster of a fish you have ever seen. Just as it is about to eat you, the dream ends.* This dream is about your fears in the future. You know that the sea is full of dangerous animals feared by nearly everybody in the same way as you fear the big kids at school. Will the bigger kids beat you up? Will you be able to escape them?

The last dream. *You are in line at school. A big boy is pushing you, trying to get in front of you. You turn around to talk to him, but no sound comes from your mouth. You can see the teacher, but she is very small and far away.* This last dream is an attempt to solve your problem. One way might be to tell the boy (who also reminds you of your big brother) that you won't stand for being pushed. But you are still too afraid of him (and your brother) to try this, and so you are unable to speak. Another solution might be to tell the teacher, but she is not available (small and far away), and you're not sure if that would be a good idea, because every time you told your mother about your brother, your brother would get you for it later. If you remember this last dream, you might think about it and see if either of these courses would work in real life. At least now, using your dreams as a basis, you have some idea of what you might do, and you could ask for some advice. Action is a lot better than feeling like a baby in a bathtub.

Unfortunately, even though dreaming seems to follow a pattern, we are not really aware of what happens during the night, and outside a sleep laboratory it is difficult to have such a complete record. However, problems that are not solved have a way of coming back to haunt us, and over a period of time you may be able to collect enough dreams with the same themes so that you can learn something about your problems and what you might do about them.

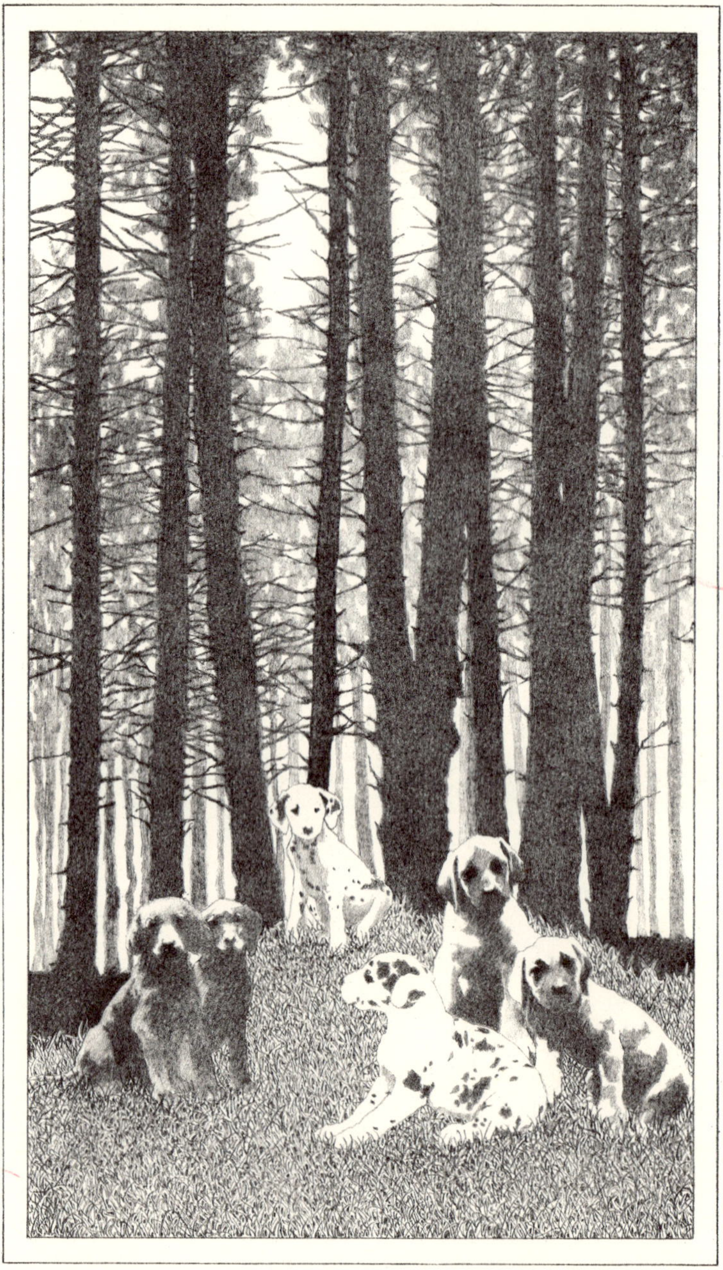

6 · *Fire and Snakes*

A snake was chasing me through the woods. I ran home. When I got to the back door I looked behind me. The snake was gone, and there were six puppies tumbling over each other instead.

Susan

The unconscious mind speaks to us in symbols, which are the pictures you "see" in a dream; in Susan's dream she "saw" a snake and six puppies. These are symbols, which were created spontaneously while Susan dreamed.

A symbol is something that stands for something else, and we use symbols in our waking life all the time. For example, an eagle may suggest power or an owl wisdom. People can be represented by symbols, too. A picture of the White House might make you think of the president. A baby carriage might remind you of your little brother. Symbols can also stand for thoughts and feelings and experiences. They are used in poetry, slang, and advertising all the time. A waterfall next to a bottle of soda may lead you to connect the soda with the idea of something cool and refreshing. Words are symbols and so are numbers. The word "apple" is not the same as a real apple you can see, smell, and taste but is a symbol for it. The number "3" stands for any three things. We use symbols in our daily life because they are convenient; they are also often poetic.

Fire, for example, is a real thing, but for as long as people can remember it has also been an important symbol. It can be positive or negative. The image of fire may suggest warmth and comfort. Many people have fireplaces in addition to central heating, and find it soothing to look at the flames. This may be a memory of the days when cave people relied on fire to keep away wild beasts.

Fire may also suggest energy and inspiration. To "get fired up" means to get excited. A person who is "hot under the collar" is angry, that is, "burned up." Often an angry person has a red face—his emotions are inflamed—and may even feel hot to the touch. Fire may also symbolize freedom, as in the torch held by the Statue of Liberty. A picture of something in flames, on the other hand, represents destruction or suffering. The sparks given off by burning logs have a resemblance to lightning, an element that may get out of control, thus inspiring fear.

Fire is also a symbol for the continuing of a tradition, as when it is passed on from hand to hand in the form of a torch before the opening of the Olympic Games. Fire is sacred in many religions. In Christianity it is considered the gift of the spirit.

Since you create your dreams and you are different from everyone else, you will have to try to find out what the symbols in them mean to you. If you dream about fire, ask yourself how you felt during your dream. Did you feel warm and comfortable? Or was your dream as frightening as Edward's, who dreamed that the world was a fiery ball, crushing people as it rolled along? At the time, Edward was "on fire" with a fever of 104°. He was uncomfortable because of the fever, and he was afraid of what might happen to him.

Or a real fire might be symbolized by something else. During the day Susan had been playing in the woods with matches and that night she dreamed: "*A snake was chasing me through the woods. I ran home. When I got to the back door I looked behind me. The snake was gone, and there were six puppies tumbling over each other instead.*"

Susan knew that it was dangerous to be playing with matches. Fire (which could hurt her) became in her dream a snake (which also could hurt her). When she reached the safety of her back door, the snake disappeared, and there were six friendly puppies instead (they stood for the six people in her family). Why did Susan dream about snakes instead of fire? Freud, Jung, and most modern psychologists would agree that only Susan would know, because it is the dreamer who knows most about herself.

Perhaps the flickering tongues of fire reminded her of the flickering tongues of snakes, and in her waking life she was afraid of snakes. People fear different things: for some it may be the Wolf Man or giant monsters; for others it may be spiders or rats.

For many years, most psychiatrists believed that symbols were sexual in nature because Freud had developed an elaborate system for interpreting dreams around this hypothesis. According to Freud, any long object like an umbrella, a snake, knife, pencil, or gun represented a penis, while a box, case, or oven stood for the uterus. Freud believed that dreams of walking up and down stairs or ladders or walking down narrow streets symbolized sexual intercourse. Rooms, tables, and boards in dreams were usually women. The list of such symbols is very long (there are over one hundred for the penis), and Freud reinforced his argument by saying that many of these words were used by people outside their dream life.

In interpreting Susan's dream, Freud might say that the snake represented Susan's father's penis, and she was afraid her father might punish her because she had done something forbidden. He might also say that Susan was afraid of being (wished to be) raped by her father, and the puppies were the babies she would like to have by him.

Jung did not agree with Freud that all symbols

had sexual meanings. Jung might say that the snake in Susan's dream was an archetypal symbol of evil. When Susan was in the woods playing with fire, she was experimenting with being independent of her family, just as Adam and Eve had defied God, their father, in the Old Testament. Their downfall was also caused by a serpent, an ancient symbol of evil. They were expelled from the Garden of Eden for their disobedience; fortunately Susan was able to return to her family.

Erich Fromm, a psychoanalyst who was born in Germany in 1900 (the year Freud's *Interpretation of Dreams* was published), does not believe in the existence of Jung's inherited collective unconscious. Like many modern thinkers, he prefers to call symbols such as fire and snakes *universal symbols,* which may also have special "accidental" meanings for different people. Accidental meanings are created out of a moment or a happening and a symbol is made up for it. Susan may be afraid of snakes and fire because she was taught they can be dangerous. Even though many people dream about fire, it will have a personal meaning for each of them.

In the second part of Susan's dream about the puppies, they made her feel safe because they are warm, cuddly, and harmless. The latent content of Susan's dream was about fear and safety even though the details were interpreted differently. In a sense, all these interpretations of her dream are correct; but only Susan, on pondering them, would be able to know which is the closest to the truth for her. In the same way, only *your* feelings about *your* dreams will help you understand them and the latent meaning of the symbols.

You can buy books with exotic names like *The Egyptian Dream Book,* which list dream subjects and their meanings. These books can be fun, but they are worthless as guides to the meaning of your dreams because there's no such thing as one list of symbols and their meanings which is true for everyone, everywhere. If you wish to understand your dreams you must try to decipher the meanings based on your own experience and feelings.

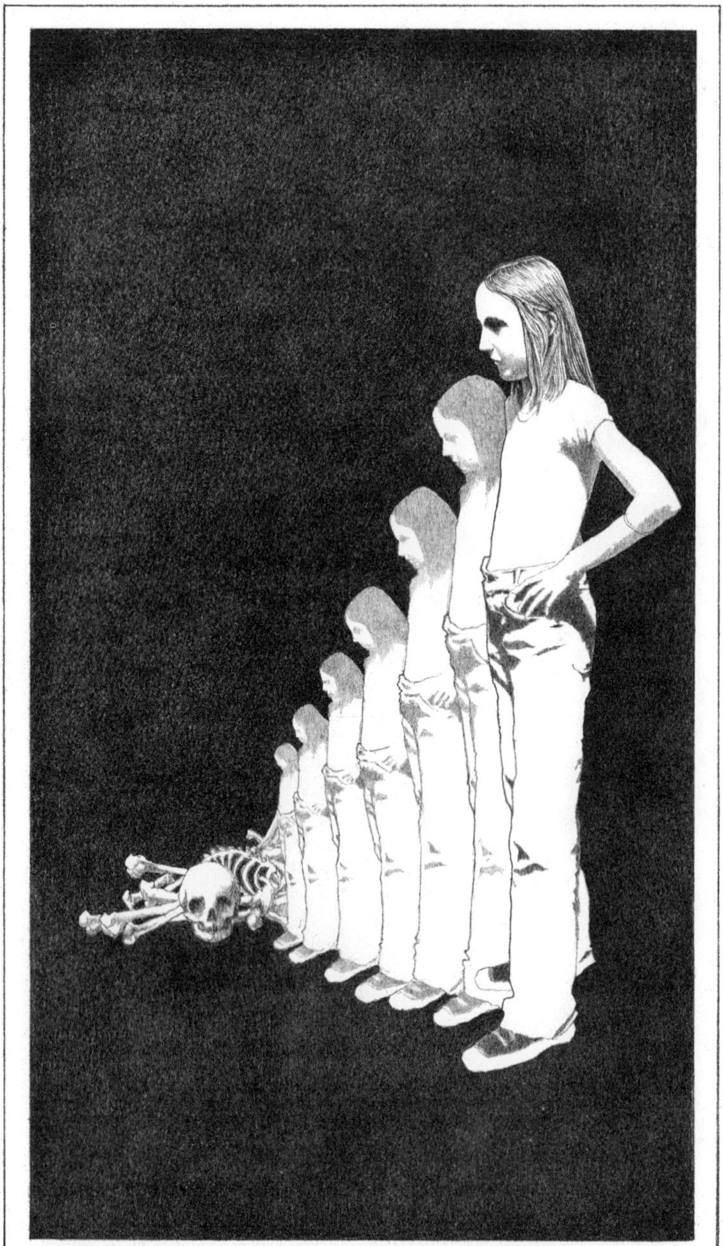

7 · Pictures on Water

I was visiting my friend Louise, who was sick. All at once Louise began to shrink until she was only an inch long. Then it was the next day, and I went to visit Louise again. Louise's mother asked me if I would like to go to the supermarket to see Louise. At the market we found a small pile of bones in a deep-freeze marked "Louise." As we watched, the bones assembled themselves into a girl until she broke out of the freezer.

Helen

The Greek philosopher Aristotle once said that dreams were like "pictures on water, pulled out of shape by movement." Even when a dream is clear and vivid, once you're awake it seems to fade around the edges and sometimes loses its shape. Although we dream in color, we often remember dreams in black and white. The way you remember your dreams and describe them is a form of distortion called secondary revision. When we recall a dream, we frequently do not remember it accurately, and we try to give it a logical order it may not have had. Also, there can be some parts we may not wish to tell anyone (including ourselves), and so we repress or "forget" them.

Dreams are distorted in other ways, and this is why they are often bizarre. Dreams communicate by way of images and bring to mind the old Chinese saying "A picture is worth a thousand words." A dream is like a rebus, a puzzle where "I" may be represented by an eye, "can" by a tin can, "swim" by a view of someone paddling in the water. A rebus is a pictorial way of presenting ideas; it is similar to the way the mind works when we are dreaming. Economical and often ingenious, the images in our dreams make poets of us all while we sleep, even though we may not always be able to "read" our own "poetry" when we are awake.

Helen's dream is a good example of how economical dreams can be. *"I was visiting my friend Louise, who was sick. All at once Louise began to shrink until she was*

only an inch long. Then it was the next day, and I went to visit Louise again. Louise's mother asked me if I would like to go to the supermarket to see Louise. At the market we found a small pile of bones in a deep-freeze marked "Louise." As we watched, the bones assembled themselves into a girl until she broke out of the freezer."

If we study Helen's dream we see that a lot is happening in the short space of one dream. Helen is in three places: Louise's room, Louise's house, and the supermarket. The drama takes two days. Louise shrinks, turns into frozen bones in a deep-freeze, and is reassembled. It is as if Helen is trying to work out a problem. The dream seems to be about Louise, who is sick, and Helen's reaction to her being ill. This is the manifest content of Helen's dream.

To discover the latent content of the dream, we should first of all ask, "Who is the dream really about?" Neither Louise nor Helen is really sick. Does Helen fear that Louise will get sick, or is she afraid that she herself will get sick? Or does Helen wish her friend would get sick for some reason—perhaps she's angry at her? We can't know the correct answers to these questions until we find out, as Freud says, "what occurs to the dreamer."

When we spoke to Helen, she admitted that she was afraid of dying. Her grandmother had died in January, and Helen was troubled at the idea of her grandmother's coffin being buried in the ground, under the wintry snows. Death was on Helen's mind, but to feel that she too might die someday was so painful, even in her dreams, that she displaced her possible death onto her friend, with whom she had had an argument that day.

Helen's parents had told her that when you died,

it was the end, there was nothing after that. In her dream, Helen watched as Louise shrank until she was almost nothing. This feeling was also too frightening for Helen, and she could not accept it.

The next day (in her dream), hoping to find reassurance, she arranged to return to Louise's house and speak to her mother. Louise's mother was a stand-in, a displacement, for Helen's own mother. People often do not dream about their parents or other people who are close to them. Instead their feelings are displaced onto other persons who in some way remind the dreamer of parents, brothers and sisters, or friends. Louise's mother took Helen to see Louise in the supermarket, which is a place for food and represents security and being taken care of. There was Louise, neatly packaged as frozen bones. Death is cold, and people (Helen's grandmother) are put away under the snow when they die.

Helen does not want to believe that death is final. This is an extremely painful feeling for her. When Louise comes back to life, Helen is reassured, and the dream ends.

Freud has said that dreams are distorted in two principal ways: condensation and displacement. In Helen's dream, time, space, and events were condensed, and people stood for more than one person at a time (Louise's mother was really Helen's mother; Louise was really Helen *and* Helen's grandmother). Freud might say the dream was distorted to protect Helen from feeling painful emotions. It was also a wish-fulfillment dream: at the end, Louise was alive, which meant to Helen that death is not the end. To make it more bearable, all these terrible things happened to someone else other than the dreamer.

In addition to using pictures, the mind also relies on word play to communicate messages. In Helen's dream, the deep-freeze stood for a snow-covered grave. Many other phrases associate cold and death, perhaps because a dead body is cold to the touch. Cold can also mean without feeling, as in cold-hearted; the cold, cruel world; a cold fish. Perhaps Helen felt that Louise had been "cold" during the argument. Such ideas might be represented in dreams by using ice or snow. Jackie dreamed she was standing barefoot in the snow, while her friends went to a party. Jackie was "out in the cold," and she had "cold feet" about asking to join her friends.

Sometimes dreams use puns, as when Walter was sad and dreamed about a whale (*whale* equals *wail*). Or a word can describe a person. Roger dreamed he had an imaginary playmate named Bongo, who played bongo drums all the time. Looking for the meanings of words and phrases in your dreams can be a lot of fun. It is truly wonderful how inventive we can be while we are sleeping. For now, think about some expressions you hear all the time and consider what they mean. What expression would fit this dream?

Dan dreamed he was flying around his apartment and felt "a tremendous sense of power." Was he "flying high"?

A dream about fog? Perhaps the dreamer is in a fog about what is happening. His thoughts are cloudy, fuzzy, gloomy?

A dream about a fish? Is something "fishy" happening?

At last we're beginning to understand. A comic-strip artist might show a light bulb lighting up. Someone else might say, "The dawn is breaking," or "The clear light of day is falling upon the problem." Sunny thoughts are happy thoughts, as a rule. Our language is full of such clichés, and with good reason: they are extremely expressive.

Words and names can also be condensed. Dracula and Godzilla could become a dream monster called Draczilla. Numbers may be important. If you dream about numbers, see if they could stand for a specific date or try adding and subtracting them until a meaning is revealed. Dorothy dreamed she was repeating the word "triceps" while making "three sand pies." Unfortunately, she had no idea why she dreamed of three. In another dream, she dreamed about the numbers 513 and 531 (as times of day). Three times three is nine. Five, one, three add up to nine. "Now I know. Nine is my lucky number, because I was born on the ninth," she said. "I think I would like some good things to happen, but I don't know what they are."

Dreams have a special "grammar," too. "Up" in a dream can mean "down," as when Mimi climbed all those steps that she really wanted to go down. Renée dreamed she went to the market to get some doughnuts and was *"in the store, looking all around. There were millions of different kinds of doughnuts. I looked, but there weren't any."* Even though there were doughnuts, Renée was telling herself through her feelings in the dream, "No doughnuts." When you feel frustrated in a dream, a conflict of will is involved. We might mention that Renée was on a diet and wasn't supposed to eat doughnuts!

It is also important to look carefully at the symbols in your dreams, because *how* you choose to visualize something is a clue to what it means to you. For example, if your mother appears in a dream as herself, this is a denotative symbol; that is, "mother" denotes a specific person. If you dream about a cow, it may be a symbol for your mother, who gives you milk and other nourishment. If you dream about a woman with a vacuum cleaner, you may be thinking of your mother as a housekeeper. If you dream about a queen, you may be thinking of your mother as regal and elegant and perhaps a bit distant. In other words, when metaphorical symbols such as these appear in your dreams, you should first try to find out who the real person is behind the symbol and then ask yourself how you feel about the way the dream represented that person. This in turn will provide the clue to understanding how you feel about the person behind the symbol.

Always remember that you are the person who created your dream, and you know best how to interpret it. As Aristotle said, the best interpreter of dreams is the person who can "grasp similarities," and only you know what they are. But remember too that we all need the help of the different kinds of techniques mentioned in this book. Dream interpretation is a skill, and like any other skill it requires instruction and lots of practice.

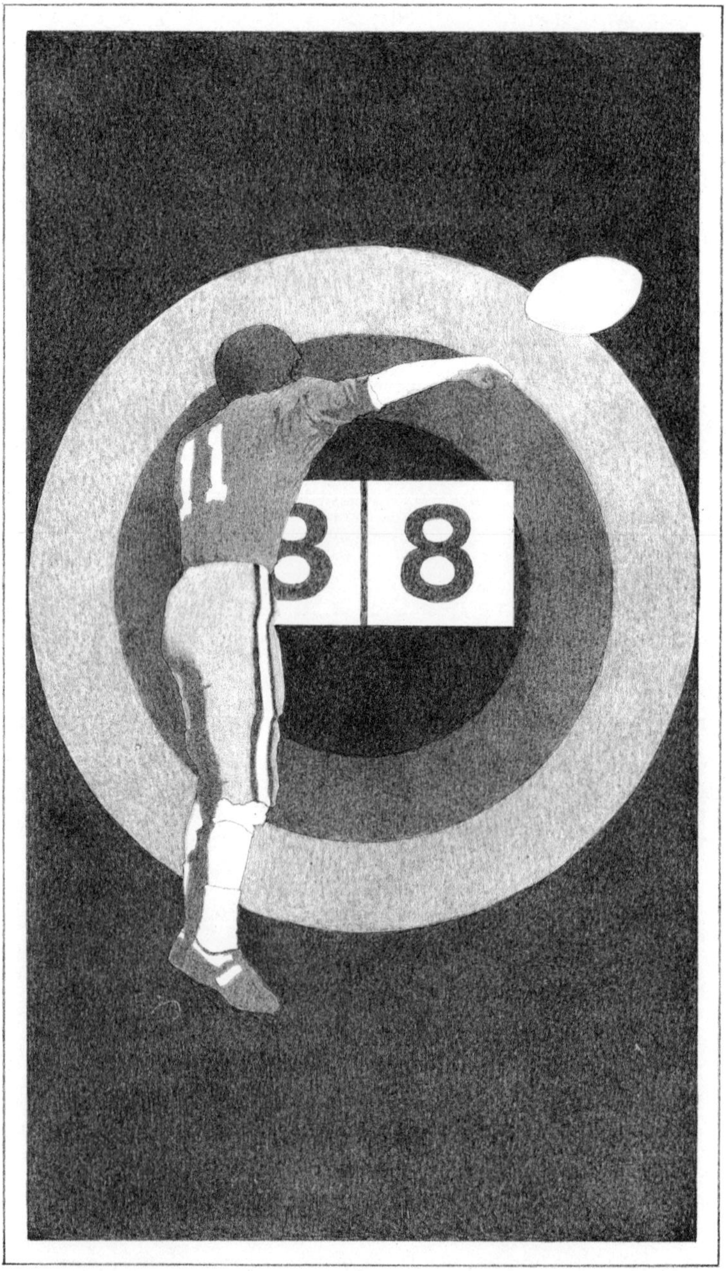
11
88

8 · Living Is Not Easy

I ran 75 yards for a touchdown. The score was tied. I got the ball again and ran 45 yards for another touchdown. My school won the game, and I felt like a big football star. Everyone congratulated me. My girl friend kept telling me that I was wonderful. My coach told me that I would be a big star someday.

John

John's wish-fulfillment dream was fantastic: "I ran 75 yards for a touchdown. The score was tied. I got the ball again and ran 45 yards for another touchdown. My school won the game, and I felt like a big football star. Everyone congratulated me. My girl friend kept telling me that I was wonderful. My coach told me that I would be a big star someday."

John had what he wanted most in one dream, and he felt very good about it.

And then there was Jim, who was walking through the jungle in his dream, *"and snakes were all around. I had a forked stick and a snake book with me. The forked stick was so I could pin down the snakes, and the snake book was so I could tell which ones were poisonous, because I was scared. I caught a python and pit viper and sold them at the Serpentarium."* This dream is a little more complex than John's dream. Jim managed to capture dangerous snakes and sell them, but more important, he went about his task with foresight and confidence (the stick and the book), overcame his fear of poisonous snakes, and earned some cash.

Wish-fulfillment dreams may turn out unhappily. Tom dreamed that he saved up all his money for a dragster. *"I bought it and then I raced it. The engine fell out in the middle of the race. I cried real hard."* In another dream a couple of years later, Tom dreamed that he got everything ready for a trip. *"I bought new clothes, polished the car, and saved extra spending money. Then, in the morning, the family started out while it was still dark. As we backed the car out of the driveway, a huge truck came tearing toward us—a crash was inevitable. I woke up."*

What had started out to be fun for Tom became disastrous. It would seem that Tom has the feeling that he won't get what he wants—or if he does, something will happen to take it away. His dragster's engine will fall out; his family's car will be hit by a truck.

Kathy dreamed she was at a dance. *"I was dressed in a beautiful dress and was surrounded by fellows who wanted to dance with me. Just as I was about to dance my mother called me away and everyone laughed."* This is another wish-fulfillment dream that turned out unfortunately.

Why does this happen? There are various reasons, which depend on what is happening in a person's life. It may be that Tom has suffered so many disappointments that he has very little faith in the future working out for him. Kathy may have a critical mother who makes her feel unconfident, so that even when she is feeling good, her mother comes along to spoil things. Or she may not feel she has "permission" to be happy.

Dreams are a reflection of our emotions. We may be feeling happy, sad, frightened, or angry during the day, but we "forget" it. At night the feelings we "forgot" come out in the shape of our dreams. Living is not easy. We may have difficulties with our parents, our brothers and sisters, our friends. We can both hate and love our parents at different times. Frequently, we are jealous of our brothers and sisters. And often our friends do things that make us angry. These feelings can be frightening because we all are afraid of losing love and esteem. It is very human to push unpleasant feelings aside, feelings we do not know how to handle, feelings we may not even know we have.

Emotions that were only half felt during the day may reappear that night in a dream, sparked by some trivial incident or scene. It is as if the mind were rounding out or finishing something that was not completed. This day residue becomes part of our dreams every night.

One day Anne and her father had a lot of fun together. They had gone to the park, visited the zoo, and climbed a small hill, pretending it was a mountain. That was the kind of life Anne wanted, but she felt it didn't happen often enough. That night Anne dreamed that her mother was dead. *"My father and I were riding on a stagecoach pulled by two lions. We were heading out west, and I knew we would have a great time."* In talking about the dream, Anne felt guilty for dreaming that her mother was dead. But it is important for Anne to remember that this was a dream; Anne did not kill her mother or really want her to be dead. She loved her mother, but she felt her mother wasn't much fun because she spent all her time at home cleaning and cooking. Anne wanted to have good times, but it seemed this was only possible with her father. And so, in the dream, her mother was conveniently dead, and Anne and her father could do what she wished.

A guilty conscience often turns up in wish-fulfillment dreams, and sometimes in funny ways. Bobbi dreamed that she and her cousin Launie were at a corral. *"There was a beautiful horse, which the owner let me* ride. Launie rode behind me. It started to rain, and the horse got scared and ran away with us. The owner was looking for his horse, but the rain had changed its color, and so the owner let us keep it. He said if we found his horse, he would give us a reward. As we started to ride away on the horse, it began to change colors again! It looked just like it did before. The owner got real mad and said we were trying to steal his horse. He called the police and they put us in jail forever."

Bobbi wanted a horse of her own more than anything. She knew it would be wrong to steal one, and so in her dream she arranged it so that the horse "ran away" with her and Launie. Then the rain changed the horse's color, and the owner couldn't recognize it. Neither of these events was Bobbi's fault. She hadn't done anything wrong. But her dream alibi wasn't strong enough to appease her conscience, and her guilt feelings surfaced in the dream at last. The horse mysteriously changed colors again. (Her conscience wasn't going to let her get away with stealing.) The owner called the police and put the girls in jail "forever." Bobbi knew that that was what happened to thieves. In our dreams, a policeman is often a symbol for our conscience.

A guilty conscience may show up in another way. George dreamed he was going to bed. "*My mother came into the room to tuck me in, as she always did. She was wearing a nightgown, and when she bent over to kiss me goodnight, her breasts fell out of her nightgown. She pulled down the sheets and got into bed with me. I felt very anxious. Mother kissed me, and we started to have intercourse. Just then a crowd of angry people appeared around the bed. I felt ashamed and tried to push myself away from my mother. Then I woke up and found I had had an emission. I felt very mean and sad. I could not face my mother all day."*

Nocturnal emissions or "wet dreams" are normal and happen to most boys as they grow up. Many boys and girls dream of having sexual intercourse with members of their family. For George, sexual feelings are exciting and embarrassing, and he feels guilty about having them—especially about his mother. He tries not to think about sex, but because he is a normal boy, it is on his mind. His mother is the woman he loves most and knows best. Her body is exciting and mysterious. George doesn't feel ready to have intercourse with a girl friend—he doesn't even have one. Therefore, he has chosen his mother. (Some boys dream of having intercourse with their sisters; girls dream of sexual relations with their fathers or brothers.) However, since incest is condemned by society, George feels guilty about his feelings toward his mother.

In his dream, George felt anxious at first, but he partially overcame his feelings of guilt by having his mother seduce him. Then his conscience grew stronger. A crowd of people (society) rebuked him. When he awoke, he felt so ashamed that he could not face his mother all day, even though in actual life he had done nothing wrong; when a dream feeling persists into the day, it is called night residue.

There is nothing dangerous or bad about having sexual dreams; they are a normal part of growing up. George's dream about his mother is his dream, and he should not feel ashamed of loving his mother. Someday he will fall in love with another woman, and his dreams are a way of preparing him for the future.

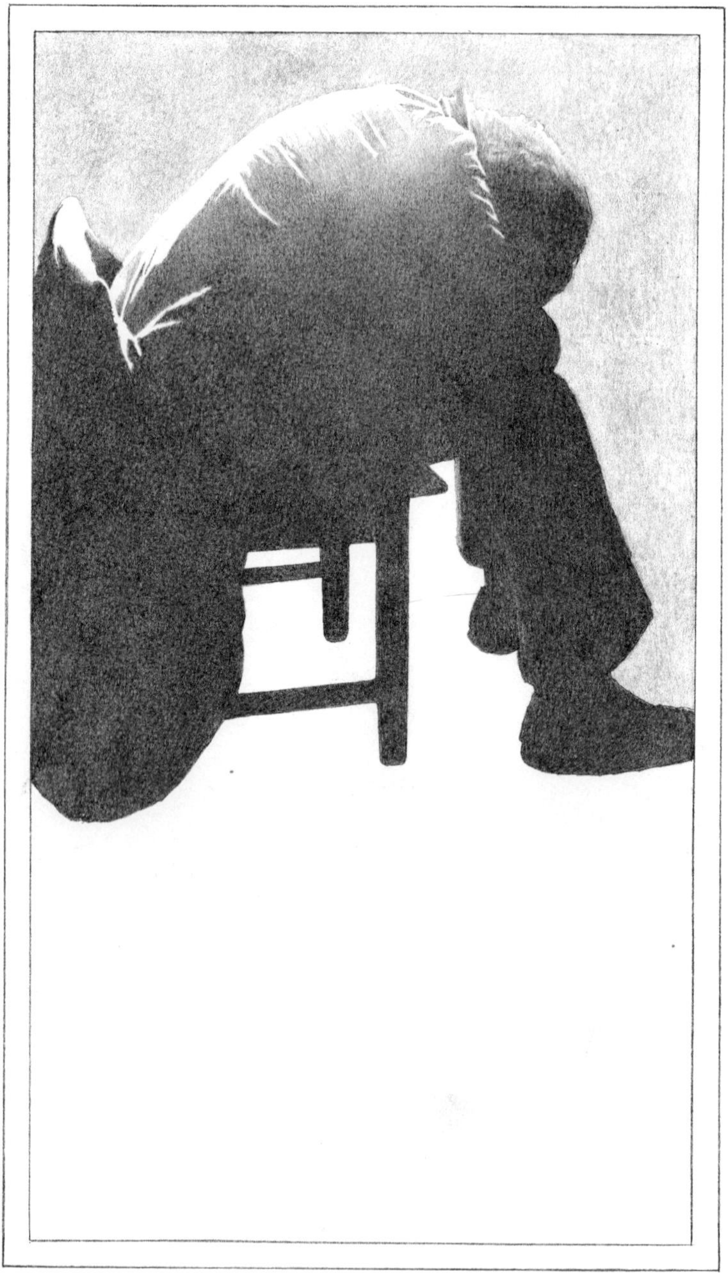

9 · Fears in the Night

I was driving a car and ran over my friend Peter in the street. I woke up feeling sort of crazy—like I might be going crazy or something. I felt I might be a potential murderer, and that was frightening.

Solomon

The dictionary defines a nightmare as a fiend or incubus (*mare* means incubus or demon) formerly thought to smother people while they are sleeping. Years ago people did not understand dreams in the same way as we do today; they thought that evil spirits could harm them while they slept. Today, a nightmare is defined simply as a frightening dream. It is not an evil spirit; it is something in our minds that disturbs us.

Like all dreams, nightmares involve events that happened during the dream day. Watching TV one evening, Fred heard a report about a new comet. That night he dreamed that *"a man was walking down the street with a box strapped in front of him. He was laughing. He opened the box and a great big ball of fire shot up in the air and exploded. Pieces of rocks fell down; it felt like it was raining rocks. The man kept walking. He wasn't hit but everyone else was."*

The great big ball of fire in Fred's dream was the comet he had heard about on TV. When he had heard the report, he had had the flickering thought that a comet might be dangerous. This disturbing feeling stayed with him unconsciously, and it was later incorporated into his dream.

Fear is in back of nearly all nightmares. Sometimes the fear is understood simply. Richard and his family went to their summer cottage at the lake. The first night, as Richard was getting into bed, he noticed there were insects all over the floor of his room. He fell asleep quickly because he was so tired after the long drive to the lake. *"I dreamed spiders were crawling all over my body,"* said Richard. "They were disgusting. I guess when I saw the bugs on the floor I must have felt how awful it would be if they were on me. But I was too tired to do anything about them, and I just went straight to bed."

Neither Fred nor Richard was consciously frightened by the comet or the bugs, but parts of their minds were disturbed. In the dreams, half-felt fear was allowed to grow into a complete event. Some people have terrible nightmares after they have spent two hours watching a horror movie and then gone to bed. It is as if the mind had to work over the material in the movie and complete it in some way. Once this was done, the energy behind the fear a person might have felt while watching the movie was discharged.

Many people dream about ghosts, movie monsters, big animals, or horrible creatures they have never seen before. This is especially likely to happen if something disturbing or frightening is going on in the person's daily life.

Ursula was unhappy about school, and she felt her mother was not sympathetic. *"I was coming home from school,"* she said about a dream, *"and a bear started to chase me. I ran as fast as I could. It took me forever to reach my house—even though it was only a short distance away. When I got there, my mother was standing at the door, but I was locked out. I woke up screaming."* The bear was a symbol of Ursula's fear (of school), and the long distance she had to run represented a conflict in her since she felt her mother would not be of much help to her.

Young children dream about animals a great deal. Since dreaming is a form of thought, it is easier sometimes to associate people with certain animals; look at the popularity of Aesop's Fables, for example. From stories and observation (and perhaps from the collective unconscious) people learn to identify certain characteristics with certain animals. We are all familiar with such stereotypes as the silly goose, the cunning fox, the brave lion, the dirty pig, and the mischievous monkey. For some reason, Ursula found big bears to be particularly fearsome.

Zachary, on the other hand, thought that bulls were dangerous. One night he dreamed a bull was chasing him down the street. *"I ran behind my building and peeked around the corner. Then I started to run down the street, but after a while I didn't see the bull anymore so I slowed down. There was a baby carriage standing on the street. I looked in it and the bull jumped out. I woke up."*

In real life, Zachary is afraid of his father, and in his dream he has conceived a bull to represent him.

We know the bull is related to Zachary because the dream takes place around his house. For a moment Zachary thinks it might be safer to be a baby again, and so he looks into the carriage. But there is no sanctuary in the baby carriage: There is a bull. Zachary's father is strict and will not permit his son to act like a baby. Zachary feels his father is too strict, and is afraid of being punished by him. Nightmares are often about the fear of punishment or of being hurt. Zachary has pushed his feelings about his father out of his mind, he thinks, but in his dreams his emotions emerge in strange shapes.

As children grow older, animals and monsters are often replaced in their dreams by people, though again the real people they are concerned with may still be represented either symbolically or as they really are.

Disturbing emotions may be represented symbolically, too. This is especially true when we do not acknowledge or accept our feelings. Emotions do not go away if we ignore them; they turn up in our dreams.

Solomon was angry with his friend Peter, but he was afraid to express it. That night Solomon had a dream. *"I was driving a car and ran over my friend Peter in the street. I woke up feeling sort of crazy—like I might be going crazy or something. I felt I might be a potential murderer, and that was frightening."*

Solomon did not have a license—he didn't even know how to drive! He had no business driving a car, and he knew it. The dream tells us that Solomon was afraid of how much harm he might inflict on someone else if his anger (like the car) went out of control. That is why he felt he might be a murderer. Since he did not express his anger directly, it built up until it came out in a violent form. Fortunately, it was in a dream.

But emotions are real, and they are connected to what is going on in a person's life. Victor had an appendicitis attack and was in the hospital when he had this nightmare: *"I was surrounded by blackness and felt a throbbing sensation. I saw clocks coming out of the darkness. They were out of tempo with the throbbing sensation. Then I saw trains coming out of blackness, toward me but not directly at me. People were coming toward me with parts of their bodies severed. Applesauce was coming out of the severed parts."*

Victor was afraid of the operation. Would he die? In the hospital, he was surrounded by sick people. The blackness, darkness, and trains in his dream were frightening and represented dying to Victor. He thought the clocks were measuring his days. As for the applesauce, he had had it for supper on the dream day!

As we grow older and have new kinds of problems confronting us, our dreams grow more complex. Ted dreamed he was walking along the street near a university in the city. *"There was no sidewalk. It was like a dirt path. I started picking flowers. I caught butterflies and put them in a jar with holes. I caught a butterfly by the wing. All of a sudden I saw the curb of the sidewalk rise up. I let go of the butterfly. The jar fell into blackness. I pulled myself away from the edge of the curb. I wanted to stay on the curb and not go where the jar went. The jar just kept going down into the abyss. I never heard the jar fall. I tried to crawl home without letting go of the curb. I was frightened. I woke up in a sweat."*

There are many things about being an adult (such as going to a university) that frighten Ted. Growing up sometimes seems to be like falling down a bottomless hole. Ted would much rather walk down a dirt road and pick flowers and catch butterflies because that is safe. He also wants to take some risks, because that is a normal part of growing up. And so he grabs a butterfly by the wing—a symbol of freedom—but is suddenly afraid and imagines the abyss is reaching for him. Holding on to the curb represents holding on to his childhood, as does his desire to crawl home.

Nightmares are terrifying experiences—and important ones. They are also normal. They put us in touch with our deepest fears and may guide us to finding a way of dealing with our problems, if only by pointing out what they may be. We can enact in our nightmares unpleasant, intense, or deadly experiences with no danger to anyone. When the mind works through an intense emotion, energy is discharged. If allowed to build up with no outlet at all, this energy might erupt in harmful ways.

Nightmares happen to everyone. If the same nightmare occurs night after night and if the night residue seems to affect our behavior during the day, it may be a warning that we need professional psychiatric help in order to deal with a serious emotional problem. Recurring nightmares can be the most terrifying events in a person's life, and it is fairly certain that help is needed to discharge this negative energy in a therapeutic way.

Some roads may take you to very strange places, and perhaps the nightmare road is the strangest of all. There is an endless fascination in the things that frighten us, whether they are giant spiders, tomato seeds, or creatures from outer space. We may be afraid of heights or caves or water or the dark. None of us is alone in our fears. Everyone fears something, and many of us fear the same things.

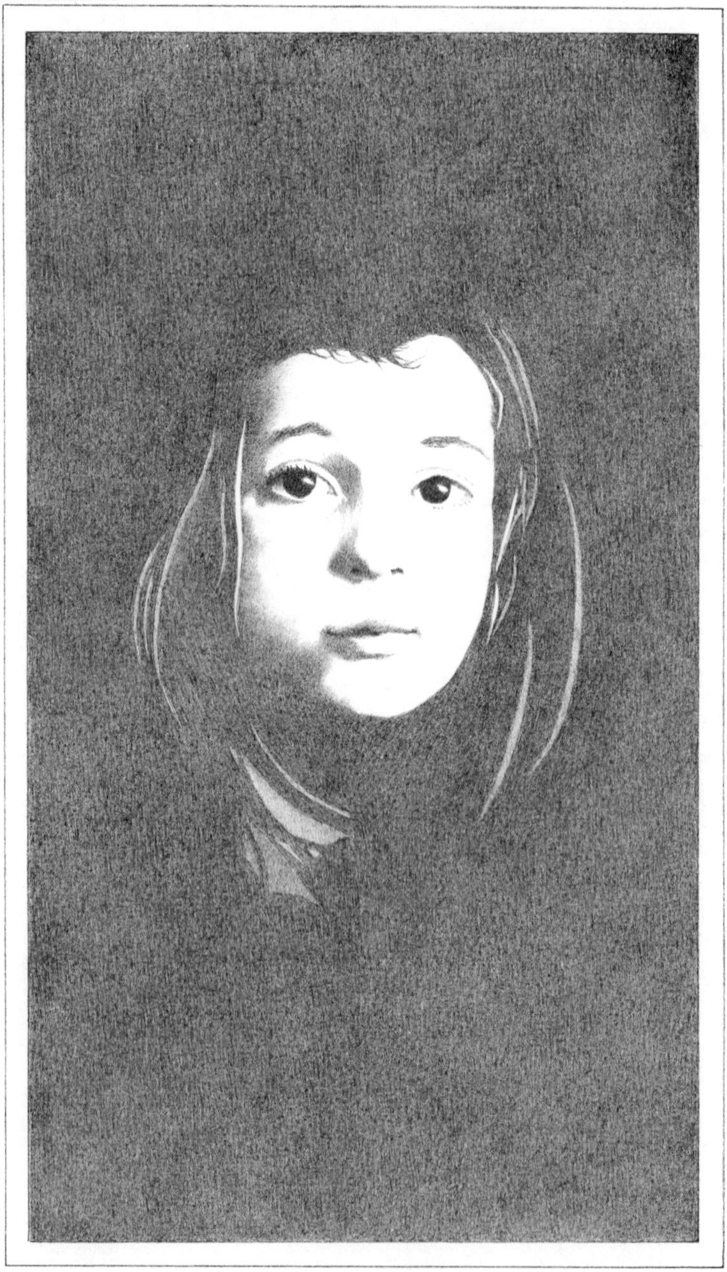

10 · Psychic Dreams

I could see a new girl in my class at school. She had long brown hair and freckles, and her name began with a "G."

Laurie

Can people communicate with each other during dreams? Can dreams predict the future? Can one person influence the dreams of another?

Many great civilizations of the past placed enormous importance on the power of dreams to predict the future. Today, after many years of mocking the idea that a person can receive information through some form of extrasensory perception (ESP)—that is, by means other than those of the normal five senses—some scientists have begun to study psychic experiences. According to Freud, sleep creates favorable conditions for telepathy, a form of ESP in which one mind communicates with another. Jung was even more inclined toward a belief in the occult, that is, the secret action of mysterious powers which had no scientific explanation. Scientists are now exploring the possibility that dreams may sometimes be telepathic.

The belief in the telepathic power of dreams is very old. The Bible contains several examples of dreams that were thought to have come telepathically from God. King Nebuchadnezzar awoke one morning unable to remember a dream that he was certain had come from God. He called throughout the land for seers and soothsayers to come to his aid. "Sire, we can only interpret your dream if you tell us what it is," they insisted. "No," the king said. "You must tell *me* the dream. I have forgotten it. If you do not help me, I will have you all killed." When Daniel heard of this threat, he prayed to God to reveal the King's dream. At last Daniel "received" King Kebuchadnezzar's dream and, to everyone's relief, interpreted it.

There are also historical instances of psychic dreams. Harriet Tubman, a slave, had prophetic dreams throughout the course of her life. One particular night she dreamed of escaping through territory she had never seen, aided by people she did not know. It was a vision of another way of life. After she had escaped slavery, she said the territory she had seen in her dream and the people who had helped her turned out to be the same as in reality and that the dream had helped guide her to freedom. She later became the most successful conductor on the Underground Railroad and helped free hundreds of slaves before the Civil War.

And in our own day, we often hear of stories like these.

One night in New York, Michele woke up from a horrible nightmare. She had dreamed of a plane crash and had heard someone screaming her name. The next morning she received a telephone call saying that her husband had been killed in an airplane accident—at the same time she had dreamed of the crash. Some people would say this was a coincidence. Others wonder whether she had had a telepathic dream: Had her husband communicated with her before he died?

Laurie dreamed a new girl with long brown hair, whose name began with a "G," was coming to her class at school. Two weeks later Gaye did appear at school and became a member of Laurie's class. Have you ever dreamed of something before it happened?

Psychic dreams like Tubman's, Michele's, and Laurie's are rarely printed in scientific journals, but they do occur. Many people report them. Psychic dreams are something scientists don't fully understand, and nobody is able to explain when and why they happen.

Scientists have been conducting experiments in dream laboratories to see if it is possible for one person to direct the thoughts of another during sleep. The procedure works as follows. First, the subject is brought to the laboratory to become familiar with the setting and the procedure to be followed. When the subject is ready to go to sleep, electrodes are fastened to his head. In another room many feet away an experimenter waits for the subject to fall asleep. When the subject has fallen asleep and is dreaming (as shown by REMs) the experimenter tries to direct the course of the subject's dreams by concentrating on a "target," usually a copy of a famous painting. When the dreaming stops, the subject is awakened and asked to describe what he has been dreaming of and to give his ideas about possible meanings. Finally, the subject's dreams are compared with the picture "sent" to him. The results so far have shown that the similarities were often significantly greater than would be expected by chance. But much more research remains to be done.

In 1960 Montague Ullman, a psychiatrist, began the planning for his mental telepathy dream laboratory. Eileen Garrett was the first subject. She was a recognized medium, which meant that she had received information many times through means other than the five senses. It was expected that because she was "psychic" she would be a good subject.

The first experiment, which was designed to test long-distance telepathy, took place on June 6, 1960. Three pictures from *Life* magazine were put in envelopes and given to Mrs. Garrett's secretary. When Mrs. Garrett started to dream, her secretary would be called; she would then concentrate on sending the picture to Mrs. Garrett telepathically. Unfortunately, the EEG did not produce tracings which indicated that Mrs.

Garrett was dreaming. However, to Dr. Ullman's surprise, Mrs. Garrett awoke and told him that she had had a dream of horses running uphill, reminding her of the chariot scene from the movie *Ben Hur*. Nonetheless, Ullman called the experiment a failure and did not call the secretary. Two weeks later Ullman learned that the target picture from *Life* had included a photo of the chariot race in *Ben Hur*—but Mrs. Garrett's secretary had never opened the envelope! Mrs. Garrett seemed to have received the target by clairvoyance (seeing things hidden from the normal human eye) rather than by telepathy. Other experiments showed that Mrs. Garrett's dreams revealed more ESP than the dreams of people who are less psychic.

Some time later Dr. Ullman's staff transferred his equipment to Maimonides Medical Center in Brooklyn and began a series of experiments there. The first studies indicated that telepathy might be affecting the contents of dreams. A person could have good telepathic dreams or dreams that had telepathic elements provided he had an open mind about the experiment in which he was taking part. Few of the people had had any memorable psychic experiences before coming to the dream lab, yet after one woman concentrated on a painting of a boxing match at Madison Square Garden, her subject dreamed of "something about Madison Square Garden and a boxing fight."

Malcolm Bessent, an English psychic, volunteered to be a subject in the Maimonides ESP dream studies laboratories. He took part in an experiment in which he attempted to dream about the judge's chosen target before it was even chosen (precognition). The experiment was considered successful because the results were statistically significant.

Psychology is the study of people, and no two people are alike. For this reason, it is especially difficult to establish facts in psychology. Psychologists describe many of their experiments with statistics. They may test hundreds of people to be able to say "the average person" does such and such, or people will do a certain act "ninety per cent of the time." They use the expression "statistically significant" to mean that the evidence is showing signs of establishing a fact.

The experiments at Maimonides Laboratory used a scale system and an independent set of judges to rate the success of each of their experiments. The judges would evaluate how close the dream of the subject corresponded with the target, the picture chosen. Many times the subject would look at the target picture after the experiment was concluded and say, "But the picture contains the same feeling I experienced. They are related." That was not good enough for the judges. The target and the subject's dream had to correspond closely for the description to be judged a "hit." From the results of the Maimonides experiments it would seem that ESP is a "normal part of human existence, capable of being experienced by nearly everyone under the right conditions."

Members of research groups around the country are also attempting personal experiments to see whether or not there is anything to the idea of telepathy. Two teachers at Centenary College in Shreveport, Louisiana, were directing their attention to a slide of a man about to fall; he was desperately holding on to the side of a tall building. Three different students had the following dreams while the instructors concentrated on the slide.

"Vivid dream where I fell off top of Sabine Hill . . . I felt myself falling, hitting the ground and bleeding—then dying."

"Climbing a rocky cliff and jumping off . . . Severed fingers crawling on floor . . . portion of hand grasping gun on floor."

"I was with two of my friends on a roof of some tall marble-like building. They were getting down by kind of falling until they caught a rainspout and then putting their feet on a bar. . . . One girl . . . fell . . . and landed perfectly on her hands."

Each of the subjects had picked up the image on the slide, demonstrating that experiments in telepathy and ESP can be undertaken even without the complicated apparatus of a laboratory.

The dream state is an altered state of consciousness in which creative forces are at work. Dreams are arranged in unique ways—taking information and conflicts and putting them together. They break with reality as we know it, and give us another kind, as rich and vivid as ordinary reality, if not more so. And, who knows? Perhaps the unconscious mind is in touch with forces outside ourselves, which, unhindered by the barriers of time and space, speak to us in dreams.

Many years ago if anyone had said that pictures could be sent through the air, they would have been thought to be foolish. Now we all take television for granted. There was a time when we didn't know about X rays or electricity. People are now doing research with ESP during the dream state and there is no way of telling what powers may be revealed in the future.

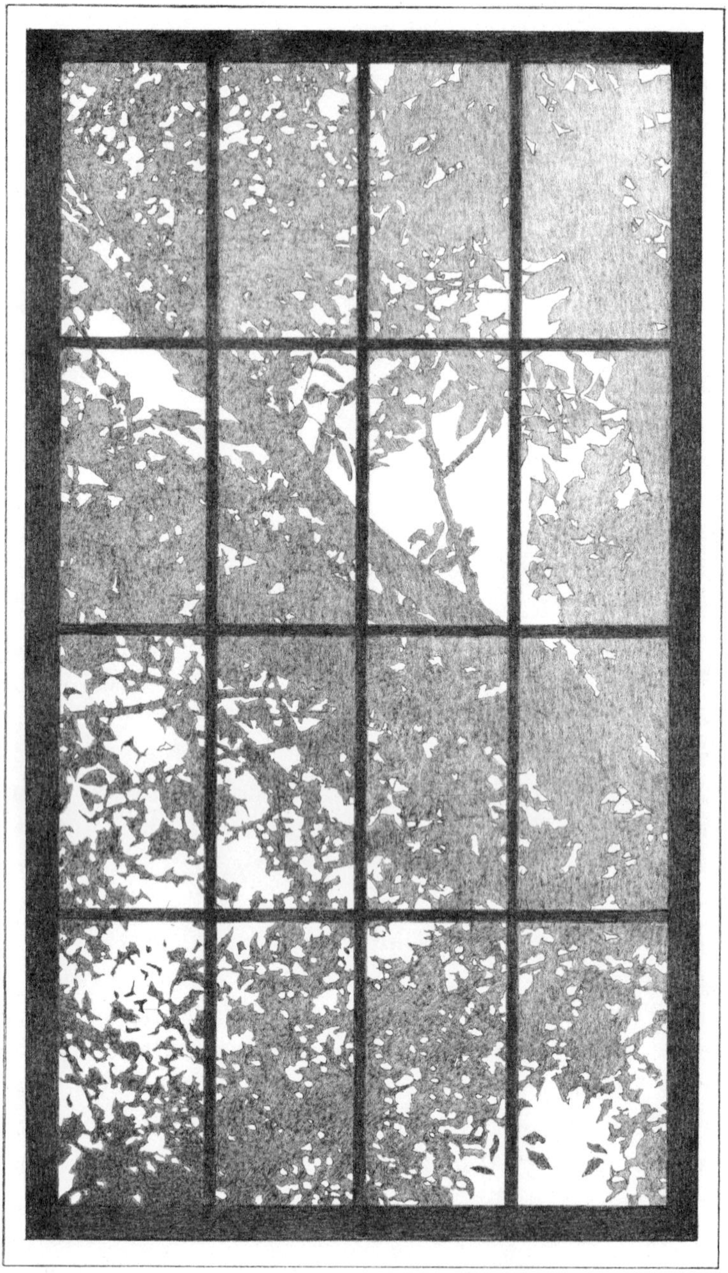

11 · The Dream People

When I looked out the window of my bedroom I saw a terribly strange and wonderful thing. It was raining; a kind of sunshower—it was light and bright out. As the rain fell on one tree the leaves turned colors. The rain became a kind of tempera or watercolor paint, and as it hit against one leaf the yellow paint would gather on the leaf and then drip down to the leaves below and mix with those colors and make wonderful bright mixtures. Because the colors were so fantastic, I took a small paper cup and held it outside to catch some. But what I got looked like only a little yellow paint in the bottom of the cup, not very exciting. It looked so fantastic on the tree, but in the cup it was just a bit of paint, and no more. I was disappointed.

Karen

Not so long ago, deep in the wooded hills of Malaysia, lived the Senoi, an isolated people who liked to be known as People of the Forest. They said there had not been a war or any violent crime in their society for the last two or three hundred years. Many Western observers believed that in human relations the Senoi were the most advanced people in the world, even though they lived in long bamboo houses mounted on stilts and supported themselves in a primitive way by farming, hunting, and fishing.

Up to a few years ago, the Senoi society was democratic, and the people lived under a system of voluntary cooperation. The Senoi did not know how to read and write. They did not send their children to schools. Instead, from an early age, children learned the Senoi art of dream interpretation.

Every day at breakfast the children told their dreams to the older members of the family. The dreams were discussed and analyzed. Later, all the Senoi adults gathered in council to report, discuss, and analyze the dreams of the older persons. The family meetings served to teach the children about dream interpretation; the community meetings were for the purpose of dream expression and the solving of personal and community problems as revealed in their dreams.

The Senoi believed that while people are growing up they create images or features of the outside world in their own minds as a way of adapting to life. For example, if a child is bitten by an insect, he may come to believe that all insects bite and then he will fear them. This one experience will have given him a false view of the insect world since many insects are quite harmless. The images created in this way may be in conflict with ourselves (that is, we have an unreasonable fear of insects) or with each other. On the interpersonal level, this may turn a person against himself or his neighbors. We can see these images in our dreams, and we must learn to recognize them so that they may be eliminated or changed.

For example, if a Senoi child reported a dream about falling, the adult would respond with enthusiasm: "That is a wonderful dream. Where did you go? What did you see?" The child would be puzzled. The dream didn't seem so wonderful to him; he was scared stiff all the time. Furthermore, he didn't go anywhere because he woke up.

"That was a mistake," the adult would answer in a serious tone. "Everything you do in a dream has a purpose. Falling is the quickest way to get in touch with the spirit world in your dreams. The next time you have a falling dream, you will remember what I am saying. The falling spirits love you. You may be frightened of their power, but relax and go on to meet them. When you think you are dying in a dream, you are receiving your own spiritual power which has been turned against you, and which now wishes to become one with you if you will accept it."

After a while, as this type of praise and advice continued, the child found that he was dreaming of the joy of flying rather than the fear of falling. An inner fear or anxiety had become joy or an act of will. As the child learned to relax in his dreams, his feelings of ill will toward the people, animals, and actions in the dream world turned to feelings of goodwill.

The Senoi had other kinds of advice for other kinds of dreams, but the ultimate goal was for the dreamer to gain control of his dream world and then his waking world. If a child dreamed of a dangerous animal chasing her, she was advised to attack the animal, calling on her friends to help. If the dreamer killed the animal in her dream, its spirit became her servant or ally. The Senoi said that a dream character was bad only if the dreamer was afraid and ran away from it.

What happened if the dreamer dreamed that a

tiger was attacking another child? The dreamer was told to warn the boy who was attacked and show him where the attack took place so that he could be on guard for it in his future dreams and kill it. The boy was then advised to thank the dreamer and to give him a present, because he was a special friend.

If, on the other hand, a child dreamed that her friend attacked her, she was advised to tell her friend about it immediately. The friend's father would tell his child that she might have offended the dreamer in some way and allowed an evil character to use her image in the dream. She, too, was advised to give a present to the dreamer and go out of her way to be friendly toward her so that this might not happen again.

When a child dreamed about floating, he was told that he must float somewhere in his next dream to find something of value. If a child dreamed about finding food, she was told to share the food. If a child dreamed he was attacking someone, he must apologize to that person and share something good with him. In this way many unconscious tensions were discharged in a constructive way. Because he was constantly encouraged to look for something new, especially in his pleasurable or loving dreams, a person became more creative as he grew older. He continually discovered new songs or dances or designs which he could share with the community on awakening.

By the time Senoi children reached puberty, they no longer had nightmares, nor simple wish-fulfillment or muddled day-residue dreams. As they grew older their dream lives became less fantastic and more like rational thinking. In dreams the dreamers solved problems, explored the unknown, had pleasant and interesting conversations, and acquired knowledge from their dream spirit guides. By using their dreams so creatively, the Senoi reduced tension in themselves and in their community and lived cooperatively in a society without crime, economic conflicts, insanity, neurosis, or psychosomatic illness.

Sadly, the Senoi no longer live so peacefully. Their communal society, which encouraged dream sharing and a cooperative way of living, was destroyed when civil war broke out among their neighbors in Malaysia.

Sharing your dreams with others is a sign of trust and love. Unfortunately, modern society is often one of violence and competitiveness, where dream sharing may be discouraged or misunderstood. If you are fortunate enough to have a sympathetic family or friends, you might wish to try systematic dream sharing with them. Or it may be possible to see a therapist or take part in group therapy.

Remember, though, there is always the danger that others will interpret your dreams according to *their* own interests, and you should never accept anyone else's analysis unless it feels absolutely right to you. And never push your interpretation of someone's dream onto him if he is at all unwilling to accept it— even if you are sure your interpretation is correct. When people do not want to hear something about themselves, it may be a sign of deep-seated conflicts inside them, and to defend their psychic integrity they will resist bringing them into the open. At this point the amateur should back away because he is in territory best left to the experts.

It is safe to analyze your own dreams because your own resistances act as a safety device to keep you from probing into dangerous areas you may not be able to handle emotionally. Again, if you feel you have serious emotional problems, try to see a therapist for help.

But we hope you will be able to relax and learn to enjoy your dreams. You may learn to use the creativity in your dreams and become more in control of your environment and come to understand your emotional reactions.

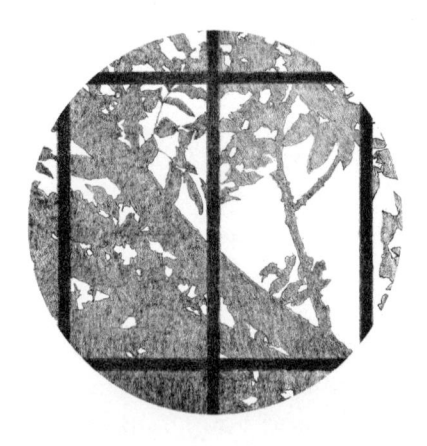

Karen's dream is a good example of this. *"When I looked out the window of my bedroom I saw a terribly strange and wonderful thing. It was raining; a kind of sunshower—it was light and bright out. As the rain fell on one tree the leaves turned colors. The rain became a kind of tempera or watercolor paint, and as it hit against one leaf the yellow paint would gather on the leaf and then drip down to the leaves below and mix with those colors and make wonderful bright mixtures. Because the colors*

were so fantastic, I took a small paper cup and held it outside to catch some. But what I got looked like only a little yellow paint in the bottom of the cup, not very exciting. It looked so fantastic on the tree, but in the cup it was just a bit of paint, and no more. I was disappointed."

Karen's dream illustrates, for example, her great desire to paint and the fact that she feels terribly frustrated by it. Shortly before she dreamed of the colored rain on the tree, she had been taking an art course at summer camp. There she saw that her amateur efforts at painting were nothing like what she wanted to do— her paper cup held only a little watery yellow paint. Her perception of herself as a failed artist blocked her from continuing to paint. The Senoi would have encouraged Karen to return to her dream, to try to capture more of the paint, to immerse herself with her creative dream spirit until she was able to bring back a new painting. At the very least, she could have tried to paint with the watery yellow paint as a start. Who knows what it might have led to?

In her waking life, Karen should continue painting until she is no longer afraid of failing. As her fear diminishes, she should become more confident in her powers until she is able to paint as surely as the rain was falling. Karen may or may not have the talent to become a great artist, but being great is beside the point. The Senoi believed that all artistic contributions were valuable, and for Karen, the pleasure and power of self-expression would be her reward.

There are many examples of people receiving inspiration from dreams. Robert Louis Stevenson's wife wrote in her diary, "I was awakened by cries of horror from Louis. Thinking he had had a nightmare, I awakened him. He said angrily, 'Why did you wake me? I was dreaming a fine bogey tale.' " He remembered enough of the dream and wrote the first version of *Dr. Jekyll and Mr. Hyde*.

Elias Howe dreamed the answer to the problem he was having in making the sewing machine work. After he dreamed of the eye-shaped holes in the tips of spears, he realized that the eye of the needle should be at the point rather than in the middle, where he had placed it originally. He hurried to his laboratory after his dream and changed the position of the eye of the needle. When he tried the machine, it worked.

Niels Bohr, the great Danish physicist, realized the structure of the atom from a dream he had. He dreamed he was on a sun composed of burning gas and planets were going by him. When the sun cooled, the planets went away. As Bohr thought about the dream he realized the planets were the electrons and the sun was the center about which they revolved.

Look at your own dreams and learn about yourself. What do you want? What are you afraid of? How might you turn fear into joy? What is holding you back from a more confident, constructive, and joyful life? If all your dreams are good, why not strive to make them even better?

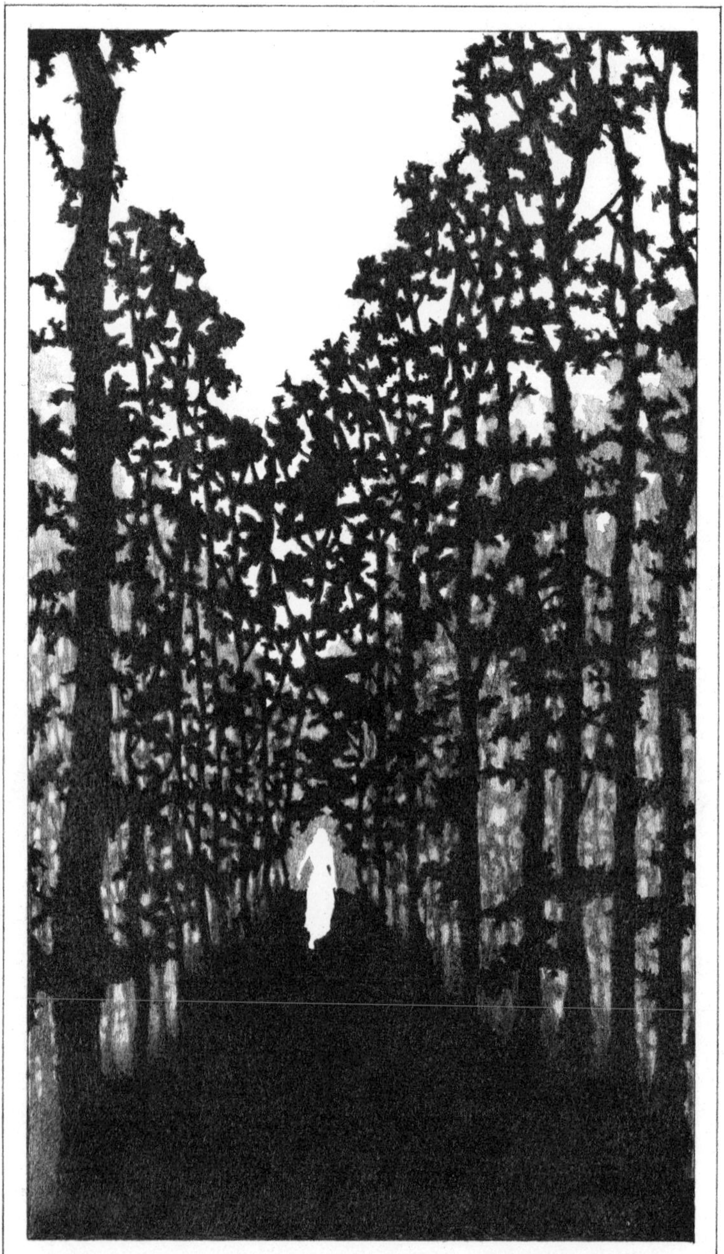

12 · A Dream Journal

Someone in a white dress was chasing me down a dark road. I was running fast and couldn't see where I was going. The person chasing me was gaining. Suddenly I couldn't go anymore. I woke up in a sweat.

Thérèse

If you would like to keep a dream journal, here is a good way to go about it. When you are getting ready for bed, place a flashlight, a pen, and a notebook beside your bed. As you drift off to sleep, say to yourself, "I am going to remember a dream tonight." This message to yourself is apt to make you wake up after you have a dream. If it doesn't, don't be discouraged. Just keep trying, and you will find yourself remembering dreams with no difficulty at all. Be patient, and don't try too hard! You will be amazed at how quickly you can learn to wake up after you dream—and remember it. In any case, if you catch your last dream of the night—the one you have just before you wake up

—you will still have enough dream material from which to work.

The best way to remember a dream is to lie still when you awake. If you jump up out of bed, the whole dream is likely to disappear. Run over the dream once in your mind before you start writing it down. It is best to write down each dream soon after you dream it. If you say to yourself, "I'll remember this dream," and wait too long, you're likely to forget it, and what you do remember will not be accurate or have as many details.

Everyone works out his or her own way to record dreams. Some people use tape recorders to take down their dreams. One psychologist who has kept a written dream journal for many years does not even open her eyes. She places a finger beside each line as she starts to write, and it guides her to the next line. She finds that opening her eyes and turning on a light is distracting. She is able to wake up and collect three or four dreams a night. You will need to find the way that works best for you. A small flashlight or a pen that lights up might be helpful.

Even if you use a tape recorder, write down each dream in a notebook. Record all that you remember, even details that seem unimportant, in your dream journal. Let your mind wander and put down any thought that occurs to you about your dreams and their possible meanings—what you did the previous day, if that seems relevant, whom you think the people in your dream represent, or how you felt during the dream. You can do this part later in the day if that seems easier than right after writing down your dream, but don't wait too long because much can be lost that way.

After you have been keeping your journal for a while, read it over and see how the various dreams fit together. See which symbols or people keep turning up. Is the same sort of situation repeated over and over?

In looking at a series of dreams, each dream should be compared to the others, and you may find that they fit together much like a giant puzzle. When you discover what one dream means, try to see how it fits in with the other dreams. If the interpretation doesn't fall into place with the other dreams, it is probably wrong. The meaning of some dreams will seem clear immediately. Start with those and go on later to the more complex dreams.

Here is an excerpt from Thérèse's dream journal.

1

I was riding a bicycle and my mother was sitting on the seat. She felt heavy, and the bicycle couldn't go very fast. I wanted her to get off, but she wouldn't.

2

I dreamed I was locked in the house and couldn't get out. My mother had taken the keys. I thought of breaking a window and jumping out, but I knew she'd be angry. So I decided to just wait.

3

My brother and I were fighting. My mother took my brother's side and said I was a bad girl and would have to be punished.

4

I forgot to take my lunch money to school. My

mother brought it to me, but she was angry that I forgot. She said I was very careless about money and would never grow up to be a responsible person. I felt very bad.

5

Someone in a white dress was chasing me down a dark road. I was running fast and couldn't see where I was going. The person chasing me was gaining. Suddenly I couldn't go anymore. I woke up in a sweat.

6

My grandmother—she looked very young—kissed me good-bye. I was going away to camp. I felt very happy, but her eyes started to fill up with tears. She said she loved me.

In one form or another Thérèse's mother appears in all the dreams. The first four dreams deal with feelings of anger and frustration. The fifth is about frustration and fear. The sixth is about love and sadness.

Thérèse is at a crucial age. She is still dependent on her mother; at the same time she wants to be independent. She both needs her mother (dreams 2, 4, 6) and would like to be free of her (dreams 1, 5, and 6).

In the first dream, Thérèse is trying to get away, but the weight of her mother on the bicycle seat is holding her back. This is a clear expression of Thérèse's conflict about being independent.

In the second dream, she is still dependent on her mother. Locked in her mother's house, Thérèse feels that only her mother has the key to free her. Thérèse is afraid to liberate herself.

The third dream demonstrates another form of dependence on her mother. She is afraid of losing her mother's love and approval and is hurt when her mother says she is a bad girl.

Thérèse feels like a little girl again in the fourth dream. Although she wants to be independent, she is forced to accept her mother's help once more, as she did in the locked-house dream. Again, her mother is angry. Thérèse is really angry at herself since she has put herself in the position where she needs her mother.

Who is the person in the white dress in the fifth dream? It is Thérèse in her graduation dress. Maturity is coming upon her, but she is fearful and isn't certain whether she can take care of herself and do the right things. Who was chasing her? Was it her mother, and did Thérèse want to be caught?

In the sixth dream, Thérèse is leaving home for camp. She wishes her mother wouldn't let her. At the same time, she feels that if her mother really loved her, she *would* let her go away. In real life, Thérèse's grandmother is warm and demonstrative, and Thérèse wishes her mother would be that way, too. That is why her grandmother looks so young; the woman in the dream was condensed from two people: loving grandmother and younger mother.

Frederick ("Fritz") Perls believed people could help themselves to become whole, or integrated, by working through their dreams.

Perls, who died in 1970, was trained as a Freudian psychoanalyst in Vienna; he came to the United States in the 1940s. Perls later developed his own methods for psychotherapy, which he called Gestalt therapy, from the German word for "whole." His method is an especially good one for recurring dreams. The dreamer should assume that every element—human, animal, vegetable, or mineral—in the dream is a part of the dreamer; no detail is too minor to ignore. Then the dreamer should recite the dream in the first person in the present tense.

After this, the dreamer should play the part of the different elements in the dream, one at a time, until something suddenly clicks. If the dreamer yawns or grows tired, it is a sign that she is resisting an important feeling and should continue. Thérèse might use Perls' technique on her first dream in this way.

BICYCLE: Oh, I can't carry two people. Why am I carrying two people? It is so hard for me to move.

RIDER: I'm sorry, Bicycle, but my mother is on the seat and she won't get off.

MOTHER: Why don't you ask me to get off? What makes you think I want to be here? You put

	me here in this dream. Take me off. You make me so angry.
RIDER:	But, Mother, I don't want to take you off.
BICYCLE:	Please get off, somebody. I'm tired.
RIDER:	I'm afraid to ask Mother to get off. I might never see her again. I want her with me.
MOTHER:	I told you that you put me here. If you want me with you why not put me on another bicycle? Then I won't hold you back.
BICYCLE:	That's a terrific idea. There's another bicycle in the garage. I bet it would love to go out for a spin.
RIDER:	O.K., Mother, come along on your own bicycle.
MOTHER:	That's much better. We can ride along together, but we shouldn't hold each other back or be forced to go where we don't want to go.
RIDER:	You're right, Mother. I was afraid that I had to drag you along or else I'd lose you.
MOTHER:	It's no fun for me to ride through life as a burden on you. I'll be at your side if you need me, but most of the time you can do well on your own.
RIDER:	It's no fun for me to ride along dragging such a weight. Let's ride together, and if we want to go separate ways we'll be able to.
BICYCLE:	Hear, hear! Let's get moving. I'm rarin' to go.

Thérèse can learn a great deal about herself and her behavior from her dream series. This might be a good time for her to discuss her feelings with her mother and explore the best way to become independent. But that is a decision she will have to make for herself.

Keeping a dream journal will help you expand your awareness of yourself and your relations with the people around you. A journal is not an end in itself; it is a bridge to make you more aware of your experiences.

It is important to remember that dreams do not offer a consistent view of the external world. They represent in pictures what your mind is thinking, and you may have more than one view about yourself or someone else. Andrew dreamed that his Aunt Mildred was loving and kind in one dream and mean and angry in another. The dreams demonstrated that Andrew had ambivalent feelings toward his aunt. We don't know whether his aunt was really mean or kind, but we do know that Andrew saw her in both ways. Perhaps he was afraid of her and wanted to see her as loving in one dream. At another time perhaps he found her possessive and restricting, so she appeared as a mean person in his dream. Each dream was consistent with what he was thinking at a certain time.

The mind is complicated, and its thoughts can't be put into a neat and tidy system, and so don't try to impose a system around your dreams where none exists. Dreaming is far different from thinking with your rational, logical mind.

A dream is a whole as it is. It is your creation. Just as nobody can think your thoughts, nobody else can dream your dreams. When you interpret your dreams, you will be led back to yourself. You have probably seen books on the shelves in drugstores or bookstores that list symbols and purport to reveal what they mean. But no book can accurately tell you what a symbol in your dream means because symbols have personal meanings. They are also part of a larger drama, and so a dream should be interpreted as a whole.

After you start recording your dreams, you can enlarge upon them—use them as taking-off places or write stories about them. Drawing a picture of a dream is an interesting thing to do. Have you ever tried to draw the stairway you're going down or the monster who is chasing you? It's fun. Plain and simple fun. Some of the greatest artists have painted pictures that seem based on dreams. Salvador Dali, de Chirico, and many others have placed dreams on canvas, from melting clocks to lonely streets. You might look for these in art books or museums to see if your feelings correspond to the feelings the artists have tried to re-create with paint.

Some people think the dreams during the hypnagogic state are the most creative. You might want to try this technique for capturing your hypnagogic dreams, which occur during daytime naps or just before you fall asleep for the night. After lying down, rest your elbow on the bed with your lower arm sticking straight up. You can then allow yourself to drift off to sleep, but as your sleep gets deeper, your muscle tone relaxes, and your arm will fall. That should wake you up, and you can take hold of what was going on in your mind.

The inner world seen and known through dreams is a fascinating place which you can never finish exploring, for you will always be dreaming new and different dreams.

Enter into the world of imagination via your dreams, and you'll see that the whole world has more to offer. Dreaming is fun when you allow the wacky and wild world of your own creation to take you places. In a short time you can live through a complex drama that might take hours to unfold on a stage. You choose the actors and set the stage. You can learn things about yourself that your conscious mind is afraid to tell you—or may not even be aware of.

We hope that you have found some answers to your questions about dreams, and we hope *The Dream Book* has given you some hints on how to know your inner desires, fears, and capabilities. A good part of your life is spent in dreaming. Why not make the most of it?

For Further Reading

Hall, Elizabeth. *Why We Do What We Do.* Boston: Houghton Mifflin Company, 1973.

Hirsch, Carl S. *Theater of the Night: What We Do and Do Not Know about Dreams.* Chicago, New York, San Francisco: Rand McNally & Company, 1976.

Hyde, Margaret O., and Forsyth, Elizabeth H. *Know Your Feelings,* New York: Franklin Watts, 1975.

Kastner, Jonathan and Marianna. *Sleep.* New York: Harcourt, Brace & World, Inc., 1968.

Kettelkamp, Larry. *Dreams.* New York: William Morrow & Company, 1968.

LeShan, Eda. *Learning to Say Good-By: When a Parent Dies.* New York: The Macmillan Company, 1976.

Rose, Karen. *In the Land of the Mind.* New York: Atheneum, 1975.

Silverstein, Alvin, and Silverstein, Virginia. *Sleep and Dreams*. Philadelphia and New York: J.B. Lippincott Company, 1974.

Sources

Bettelheim, Bruno. *The Uses of Enchantment.* New York: Alfred A. Knopf, 1976.

Calder, Nigel. *The Mind of Man.* New York: The Viking Press, 1971.

Caligor, Leopold, and May, Rollo. *Dreams and Symbols.* New York: Basic Books, 1968.

Campbell, Joseph (ed.). *The Portable Jung.* The Viking Press, 1971.

Faraday, Ann. *Dream Power.* New York: Coward, McCann & Geoghegan, 1972.

———. *The Dream Game.* New York: Harper & Row, 1974.

Foulkes, David. *The Psychology of Sleep.* New York: Charles Scribner's Sons, 1966.

Freud, Sigmund. *The Interpretation of Dreams.* New York: Basic Books, 1955.

———. *An Outline of Psychoanalysis.* New York: W.W. Norton, 1949.

Fromm, Eric. *The Forgotten Language.* New York: Grove Press, Inc., 1957.

Garfield, Patricia. "Keeping a Longitudinal Dream Record." *Psychotherapy: Theory, Research and Practice.* Vol. 10, No. 3, Fall 1973, pp. 223–8.

Gutheil, Emil. *The Handbook of Dream Analysis.* New York: Liveright Publishing Company, 1951.

Hall, Calvin S. *The Meaning of Dreams.* New York: McGraw-Hill, 1966.

Jones, Richard M. *The New Psychology of Dreaming.* New York: The Viking Press, 1970.

Jung, C.G. *Dreams.* Princeton: Princeton University Press, 1974.

———. *Man and His Symbols.* Garden City: Doubleday, 1964.

———. *Memories, Dreams, Reflections.* New York: Random House, Inc., 1961.

Krech, David; Crutchfield, Richard S.; and Livson, Norman. *Elements of Psychology.* New York: Alfred A. Knopf, 1974.

Olsen, Paul, et al. *Emotional Flooding.* New York: Penguin Books, 1977.

Piaget, Jean. *The Child's Conception of the World.* Totowa, N.J.: Littlefield, Adams, and Co., 1965.

Stevenson, Robert Louis. *Dr. Jekyll and Mr. Hyde.* New York: Pocket Books, 1972.

Stewart, Kilton. "Dream Theory in Malaya." *Complex.* Fall 1951, pp. 21–34.

Stewart, Walter A., and Freeman, Lucy. *The Secret of Dreams*. New York: The Macmillan Company, 1972.

Ullman, Montague, and Krippner, Stanley, with Vaughan, Alan. *Dream Telepathy*. New York: The Macmillan Company, 1973.

Index

Adler, Alfred, 49–50
Alice in Wonderland (Carroll), 33, 34
Animals
  dreaming, 43–44
  in dreams, 83–84
Archetypes, 30
Aristotle, 65, 71
Aserinsky, Eugene, 39
Atom, structure of, 104

Bessent, Malcolm, 93
Bohr, Niels, 104
Browne, Sir Thomas, 39

Chirico, Giorgio de, 115
Chwang-Tse, 16
Clairvoyance, 93
Collective unconscious, 30, 33
Condensation, 68

Dali, Salvador, 115
Daydreams, 15–16
Déja vu phenomenon, 51
Dement, William, 39

Dialogue technique, 35
Displacement, 68
Dr. Jekyll and Mr. Hyde (Stevenson), 104
D-state, 42

Electroencephalogram (EEG), 40
Extrasensory perception (ESP), 89, 93–95
Eye movements, 40–45

Fantasies, 16
Fire, 58–60
Foulkes, David, 44, 50–51
Free association, 22–23, 25
Freud, Sigmund, 22–26, 29, 50, 60, 61, 67, 68, 89
Fromm, Erich, 61

Garrett, Eileen, 92–93
Gestalt therapy, 112

Hercules, 33
Homer, 39
Howe, Elias, 104
Hypnagogic state, 41–42, 115

The Interpretation of Dreams (Freud), 26

Jonah, 33
Jung, Carl, 29–36, 50, 60–61, 89

Kleitman, Nathaniel, 39

Laing, R. D., 22
Latent content of dreams, 61, 67

Maimonides Medical Center, 93–94
Manifest content of dreams, 24, 67

Nebuchadnezzar, King, 90
Nightmares, 17, 81–87
No Rapid Eye Movements (NREMs), 42, 44–45, 50
Numbers, 70

Pasternak, Boris, 31
Perls, Frederick, 112
Pinocchio, 33
Precognition, 93
Puberty rites, 30–31
Puns, 69

Rapid Eye Movements (REMs), 41–44, 50, 92

Remembering dreams, 50–51, 65, 107–108
REMs. *See* Rapid Eye Movements

Senoi society, 97–101, 103
Sewing machine, 104
Sexual dreams, 78
Sexual symbols, 60–61
Sleep laboratories, 39–43, 91–93
Sleeping stages, 41–45
Sleepwalking, 45
Stevenson, Robert Louis, 103–104
Symbols, 57–62, 70–71, 77, 83, 115
  fire, 58–60
  sexual, 60–61

Tape recorders, 108
Telepathy, 89–95
Tubman, Harriet, 90

Ullman, Montague, 92–93
Unconscious, 17–18, 22, 23, 26, 30, 33, 36, 95

Walkabout, 31–32
Wish fulfillment, 23, 45, 73–76
Word play, 69–70

Library of Congress Cataloging in Publication Data

Litowinsky, Olga. The Dream book.
Bibliography: p. Includes index.
SUMMARY: Highlights various approaches to dream interpretation with emphasis on the work of Sigmund Freud, Carl Jung and others.
   1. Dreams—Juvenile literature. 1. Dreams I. Willoughby, Bebe, joint author. II. Diamond, Donna. III. Title.
BF1091.L56   154.6'34   77-22922 • ISBN 0-698-20427-1

Olga Litowinsky has always been interested in dreams and their meanings. After reading Freud's *The Interpretation of Dreams* at age 17, she began to delve into the significance of her own dreams.

A graduate of Columbia University, Ms. Litowinsky is an editor of children's books at the Viking Press. A native of Belmar, New Jersey, Ms. Litowinsky lives in Brooklyn Heights and has recently published her first novel, *The High Voyage*.

Bebe Willoughby grew up on Martha's Vineyard, an island off the coast of Massachusetts. She received a B.A. at Goucher College and an M.F.A. at Columbia University.

Ms. Willoughby lives in New York City, where she has worked in both advertising and publishing. Over the years the author's interest in dreams has resulted in a sizeable collection of her own dream journals. They are, she says, an invaluable way of keeping in touch with your deepest feelings.

Donna Diamond has illustrated five books for children, including *The Boy Who Sang the Birds*, by John Weston, and *Ann's Spring*, by Daniel Curley.

The artist graduated with a B.F.A. from Boston University and attended the School of Visual Arts in New York. Ms. Diamond now lives and works in New York City.

*The display and text type
are set in Palatino.
The art was reproduced
with a contact method.
The artist used
pencil on mylar.*

	DATE DUE		
MAR 30 '90			
FEB 22 '91			
MAR 4 '93			
DEC 15			
MAY 13 '94			
MAY 22 '96			
		/	

```
154.6                              21326
Lit
```

Litowinsky, Olga

The dream book

Riverside High School
Library